THE TWELVE

THE LIVES OF THE
APOSTLES AFTER CALVARY

D0973933

7.95

THE TWELVE

THE LIVES OF THE
APOSTLES AFTER CALVARY

by
C. Bernard Ruffin

OUR SUNDAY VISITOR, INC.
HUNTINGTON, INDIANA 46750

Cover design by DesignMarks, Inc.

LIBRARY OF CONGRESS CATALOG CARD NO.: 83-63168
INTERNATIONAL STANDARD BOOK NO.: 0-87973-609-7

Published, printed and bound in the U.S.A. by
Our Sunday Visitor, Inc.
200 Noll Plaza
Huntington, Indiana 46750

609

Acknowledgments

Scripture texts used in this work are taken from the *New American Bible,* © 1970 by the Confraternity of Christian Doctrine, Washington, D.C., and are used by license of said copyright owner. No part of the *New American Bible* may be reproduced in any form without permission in writing from the copyright owner. All rights reserved.

Other biblical quotations are taken from the *King James Version* (KJV), the *Revised Standard Version* (RSV), and the *New English Bible* (NEB).

Excerpts from the historical works of Eusebius are reprinted from Eusebius, *The History of the Church from Christ to Constantine,* translated by G.A. Williamson, Penguin Books, 1965. © 1965 by G.A. Williamson. Reprinted by permission of Penguin Books, Ltd.

Excerpts from the *Apocrypha* are reprinted from the *New Testament Apocrypha: Volume One: Gospels and Related Writings,* edited by Edgar Hennecke and Wilhelm Schneemelcher. © 1959 by J.C.B. Mohr (Paul Siebeck), Tubingen; English translation © 1963 by Lutterworth Press. Published in the U.S.A. by The Westminster Press. Reprinted and used by permission.

Dedication

*This book is dedicated to
Miss Edith C. Butler,
my high school English teacher,
without whom this book
could not have been written.*

Table of contents

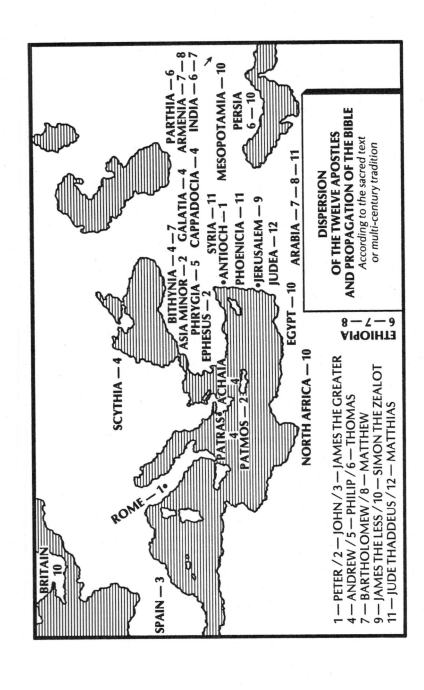

DISPERSION
OF THE TWELVE APOSTLES
AND PROPAGATION OF THE BIBLE
*According to the sacred text
or multi-century tradition*

BRITAIN — 10

SPAIN — 3

ROME — 1

NORTH AFRICA — 10

PATMOS — 4
PATRAS — 4
ACHAIA — 4

SCYTHIA — 4

BITHYNIA — 4 — 7
ASIA MINOR — 2
PHRYGIA — 5
EPHESUS — 2

GALATIA — 4
CAPPADOCIA — 4

PARTHIA — 6
ARMENIA — 7 — 8
INDIA — 6 — 7

MESOPOTAMIA — 10

PERSIA
6 — 10

SYRIA — 11
•ANTIOCH — 1

PHOENICIA — 11

•JERUSALEM — 9
JUDEA — 12

EGYPT — 10

ETHIOPIA
6 — 7 — 8

ARABIA — 7 — 8 — 11

1 — PETER / 2 — JOHN / 3 — JAMES THE GREATER
4 — ANDREW / 5 — PHILIP / 6 — THOMAS
7 — BARTHOLOMEW / 8 — MATTHEW
9 — JAMES THE LESS / 10 — SIMON THE ZEALOT
11 — JUDE THADDEUS / 12 — MATTHIAS

Introduction

WHEN I was enrolled at Yale Divinity School in New Haven, Connecticut, I attended church for the first time at Christ Church Episcopal on the Feast of St. Matthew, September 25, 1969. The rector, Father William Kibbitz, preached on II Corinthians 4:5 (KJV): "For we preach not ourselves, but Christ Jesus the Lord." His point was that we know almost nothing about St. Matthew because the apostle was much more concerned that we know about Jesus than that we know anything about himself.

This is a powerful obstacle to anyone writing about the lives of the Twelve Apostles of our Savior. None of the apostles seems to have had the slightest interest in perpetuating his own memory. Their whole being was centered on their Master, Christ, and on spreading the Good News that everlasting life was to be found through a personal commitment to Him. Even in the Gospels, the followers of the Lord were not so much concerned with writing a biography of Jesus, at least in the sense that we usually understand biography. Except for the circumstances of His birth, the evangelists told us little about Our Lord's early life up to the beginning of His public ministry in A.D. 28. The evangelists were not particularly concerned about specifying an exact chronological order for the events that they recounted, and they did not bother to tell us what Jesus looked like or what His personal idiosyncrasies were.

This was probably deliberate. To know what Jesus looked like, to know what He liked to eat and drink, how tall He was, what books He read and what He liked to do for recreation was irrelevant to the apostles. They were interested chiefly in proving that Jesus was Israel's long-expected Messiah, and that all mankind could find salva-

1

tion in Him. Only those things that would help men see Christ as their Savior interested the writers of the New Testament. As St. John declared, "Jesus performed many other signs as well — signs not recorded here — in the presence of his disciples. But these have been recorded to help you believe that Jesus is the Messiah, the Son of God, so that through this faith you may have life in his name." (Jn. 20:30-31)

It would naturally follow, since the apostles were not concerned about passing down biographical details about the Lord, that they were concerned even less about preserving information about their own backgrounds and careers. This is, however, not the only reason for the paucity of information about the Twelve. A great deal of written material must have been lost in the destruction of Jerusalem in A.D. 70, and still more during the centuries of persecution that ended only in A.D. 313 with the Edict of Milan, in which the Emperor Constantine I granted equal toleration to all religions. When, subsequently, that emperor began to support the Christian Faith and scholars were free to research and write unmolested, much valuable information was gone forever.

Before the time of Constantine, most Christian leaders had been concerned mainly with teaching the Gospel of Christ and preserving it in the face of persecution and death. Afterward, many Church leaders expressed an interest in knowing more about the people who surrounded Jesus. St. John Chrysostom (A.D. 344-407), the "golden-mouthed" bishop of Constantinople, wrote:

I wish that it were possible to meet with one who could deliver to us the history of the Apostles, not only all they wrote and spoke of, but of the rest of their daily life, even what they ate, when they walked, and where they sat, what they did every day, in what parts they were . . . where they lodged — to relate everything with minute exactness. . . .[1]

The first important author to write extensively on the history of the Church was a Palestinian prelate named Eusebius, who died in A.D. 339. For a quarter century he was bishop of Caesarea, a city which lies on the coast of what is now Israel, halfway between the modern cities of Tel Aviv and Haifa. A friend of Constantine, Eusebius, upon compiling his *History of the Church*, had access to all the documentation that still existed. The library of Bishop Alexander in Jerusalem then contained an excellent archive of Christian material, and Eusebius was able to draw upon it to quote from many works which no longer exist today. Eusebius was a careful, impartial, painstaking historian who took care to cite his sources and to indicate when he thought that a fact was questionable. He was just as interested as John Chrysostom would be a few decades later in digging for facts about the biographies of the apostles and other prominent early Christians. Unfortunately, he seems to have been somewhat disappointed with the information he was able to acquire. He was as removed in time from the days of the apostles as we are today from the time of Shakespeare, and, although many sources were available to him that have since vanished, many more had already been lost by his day.

From the writings of Eusebius, however, we are able to glean a small amount of information about the lives of the apostles. Moreover, other writers from the second, third and fourth centuries yield further tidbits of information. Among those were Papias (A.D. 60-135), bishop of Hierapolis (in what is now Turkey), a disciple of St. John, whose works, no longer extant, were quoted in fragments by Eusebius and other writers; St. Clement of Rome, (A.D. 30-97) a disciple of Peter and Paul who reigned as pope be-

3

tween A.D. 92 and 101; Irenaeus (c. A.D. 120-c. 202), bishop of Lyon (in what is now France); Clement of Alexandria (c. A.D. 153-c. 217), an eminent Greek theologian and hymnist; Hippolytus (c. A.D. 170-236), a pupil of Irenaeus and author of a number of theological works; Tertullian (c. A.D. 145-c. 221), a Latin-speaking African theologian; Origen (c. A.D. 185-c. 254), a celebrated Egyptian teacher, theologian and ascetic; and St. Jerome (c. A.D. 342-420), the celebrated Italian scholar and translator. The information these first-class scholars were able to gather is, alas, in bits and pieces, but it is all that we have that is reliable.

More extensive accounts come from various apocryphal works which first began to circulate in the second and third centuries. These documents, which include *The Apostolic History of Abdias, The Acts of Peter, The Acts of Paul, The Acts of John* and *The Acts of Philip,* are actually historical novels, almost always accepted as fictional accounts based on real events — although often teaching unsound theology. From some of these accounts it is possible to make some reasonable suppositions about the lives of the apostles. Then, too, in India there exists a substantial oral tradition, largely unknown to the West until the sixteenth century, about St. Thomas, who worked and died there.

Simply identifying all of the Twelve Apostles is a minor dilemma. One problem in identifying them precisely is the fact that first-century Jews seemed to have had comparatively few given names! In the New Testament alone there are eleven different men named Simon; six named Jude; nine Johns; six Jameses; five Josephs; seven Marys; two Philips; and even two other men named Jesus, including the terrorist surnamed Barabbas whose release from prison the Jewish mob demanded when Pilate gave them the opportunity to release the Christ. In reading Scripture, it is sometimes hard to tell who is who. The

4

apocryphal works cited above refer to Philip the apostle as well as Philip the deacon. Here again we cannot be perfectly certain whether one man or two are being identified. Eusebius recounted that there were two Johns buried in the city of Ephesus, the apostle John and one of his disciples, John the presbyter (priest), who may have edited or even written some of the material in the New Testament under the name of John. Even so, it is possible to identify with a great deal of certainty all of the Twelve.

It is important in the first place to understand the role of the apostles. It was customary for Jewish rabbis of the time to have schools of disciples. These men usually lived in a close community around their master. Not only did they receive instruction from him, they also looked after his material needs. Ronald Brownrigg, the Anglican scholar, pointed out in his work, *The Twelve Apostles*, that although there were many similarities between Jesus and the Twelve Apostles and the typical Hebrew rabbi and his followers, there were notable differences. Like most rabbis, Jesus taught in synagogues on the Sabbath. He frequently taught in parables. He was served and even financed by a circle of pious ladies, just as many of His contemporaries were. Unlike other rabbis, however, He did not confine His preaching to the synagogues, but frequently engaged in what John Wesley called "field preaching," speaking in open fields, from the rostrum of ships, in village squares and in private homes. Moreover, unlike the typical rabbi, who was sought out by his disciples, Jesus chose His disciples. Not only did they not choose Him, they were not encouraged to graduate into rabbis themselves and attain the same stature as Jesus. Perhaps most significantly, unlike students in rabbinical schools, Jesus' disciples were bound not so much to the law of Moses as to Him personally.

Next, it is important to distinguish between the terms

5

"the Twelve," "the apostles," and "the disciples." They are *not* interchangeable. "Disciple" is the broadest term, referring to all those who followed Jesus and studied under Him. The Twelve and all other apostles were disciples, but not all disciples were apostles, and not all apostles were members of "the Twelve."

"Apostle" comes from the Greek word meaning "to send." In the most basic sense, an apostle was a missionary or messenger. In the New Testament sense of the word, the apostles were the Lord's special messengers, chosen directly by Him for a special function, namely, to serve as witnesses to the Resurrection (Acts 1:22), and to proclaim to all the world how people could appropriate for themselves the effects of the Resurrection (Acts 1:8, Mt. 28:19-20). Jesus chose a group, or "college," of twelve men for this purpose. There was only one addition to this "apostolic college." After Judas Iscariot defected, the remaining eleven apostles replaced him with a man who had been a disciple since the beginning of Jesus' ministry, and who had also been a witness to the Resurrection. This was St. Matthias.

In New Testament times there were apostles who were not of "the Twelve." The Acts and other New Testament writings mentioned several such men, the most prominent of whom was St. Paul, the most important figure after Christ in sacred history. Although the risen Christ had appeared to him in a bodily vision, St. Paul had not been a disciple of Christ during the Lord's earthly ministry, and thus he was technically not one of the Twelve, although he was accepted as possessing an equal authority. St. Barnabas, too, was considered an apostle, although not one of the Twelve, probably for the same reason.

Now we must speak briefly of the Seventy (or Seventy-two) Disciples who were active in Palestine during Jesus' ministry on earth. They may have been appointed before

Jesus selected the complete number of the apostolic college. At least one man, Jude Thaddaeus, was possibly one of the Seventy Disciples before he became one of the Twelve Apostles. St. Luke, a disciple of St. Paul (but neither an apostle, one of the Twelve, nor one of the Seventy) described how Jesus appointed these men and sent them in pairs to every place he was going to visit himself.

He said to them: 'The harvest is rich but the workers are few; therefore ask the harvest-master to send workers to his harvest. Be on your way, and remember: I am sending you as lambs in the midst of wolves. Do not carry a walking staff or traveling bag; wear no sandals and greet no one along the way. On entering any house, first say, "Peace to this house." If there is a peaceable man there, your peace will rest on him; if not, it will come back to you. Stay in the one house eating and drinking what they have, for the laborer is worth his wage. Do not move from house to house. Into whatever city you go, after they welcome you, eat what they set before you and cure the sick there. Say to them, "The reign of God is at hand." If the people of any town you enter do not welcome you, go into its streets and say, "We shake the dust of this town from our feet as testimony against you. But know that the reign of God is near. I assure you, on that day the fate of Sodom will be less severe than that of such a town." ' (Lk. 10:2-12)

The Seventy Disciples were thus traveling missionaries who did the "footwork" for the Lord and for the Twelve. They were clearly subject to the Twelve, who were the direct recipients of the Lord's teachings. A writing ascribed to Hippolytus identified some of the disciples, among whom were the future apostles Jude Thaddaeus and Matthias; Cleopas (or Clopas, or Alphaeus), the father of the apostles Matthew and James the Less;

7

Ananias, who healed St. Paul in Damascus after the latter's encounter with the risen Christ; Stephen, the first Christian to die for his Faith; Agabus, mentioned in Acts as a prophet, and Linus, who succeeded St. Peter as pope.[2] In addition, there were other disciples who were not of the Seventy: Mary Magdalene, Lazarus and his sisters Mary and Martha, and the friendly pharisees Nicodemus and Joseph of Arimathea. Then there was the man known as James the Righteous, who seemed to have exerted authority equal to that of Peter, and stood in a category almost by himself. We will discuss him in a later chapter.

It is the Twelve with whom we are concerned in this book, the men, who, along with Paul and James, took precedence over all the other followers of the Lord and acted as the leaders of His Church and the custodians of His teachings after His return to heaven. It was to the Twelve, according to many of the Fathers of the Church, that He imparted the fullness of truth.

What were the names of the Twelve? There was a superficial discrepancy in their identity as they were listed by the evangelists. Matthew, Mark and Luke gave us complete lists of the Twelve. John, at different points in his narrative, named nine of the apostles. According to Matthew and Mark, the apostles were: Peter, Andrew, James (the son of Zebedee), John, Philip, Thomas, Bartholomew, Matthew (called Levi elsewhere in their Gospels), Simon Kananaios, Thaddaeus and Judas Iscariot. Luke listed ten names identical to those mentioned by Matthew and Mark. Instead of Simon Kananaios, however, he spoke of Simon the Zealot, and instead of Thaddaeus, he listed "Judas, the son of James." St. John, almost certainly referring to himself, mentioned "the disciple whom Jesus loved," and named Peter, Andrew, James (the son of Zebedee), Philip, Thomas and Judas Iscariot. There was no mention by John of Matthew, James (the son of Alphaeus) or Simon.

He did mention "Judas, not Iscariot." In addition, he named an apostle mentioned by no one else: Nathanael. The discrepancy in the catalogues of the apostles given by the evangelists occurred actually with only two names. It is beyond dispute that the apostolic college consisted of Simon Peter, Andrew, James (the son of Zebedee), John, Philip, Thomas, Matthew, James (the son of Alphaeus), Simon (called either Kananaios or the Zealot), and Judas Iscariot. The problem lies with Bartholomew, who was mentioned by the synoptic writers (Matthew, Mark and Luke) and Nathanael, who was mentioned only by John. It also lies with Thaddaeus, who was mentioned by Matthew and Mark, and "Judas the son of James," identified by Luke, and "Judas, not Iscariot," identified by John. Only the most skeptical and nitpicking of scholars would have any problem with these discrepancies. Nathanael and Bartholomew were *probably* the same man, as we shall see. Judas, the son of James, was most likely the same man as Thaddaeus. There is a possibility, however, that Nathanael, called first by Christ, might have died during Jesus' ministry, to be replaced by Bartholomew, but it is more likely that Nathanael was the given name and Bartholomew the patronymic of the same man.

From earliest times it was understood that the apostles were the embodiment of the teaching of Christ, which they handed down in an orderly manner to their authorized successors. St. Clement of Rome, the fourth pope, described by Eusebius as a man "who had seen the blessed apostles and conversed with them and still had their preaching ringing in his ears and their authentic tradition before his eyes,"[3] wrote:

The apostles received the Gospel for us from the Lord Jesus Christ: Jesus the Christ was sent from God. Thus Christ is from God, the apostles from Christ: in both cases the process was orderly and derived from the will of God. The apostles received their instructions; they were filled with conviction through the Resurrection of Our Lord Jesus Christ, and with faith by the word of God; and they went out full of confidence in the Holy Spirit, preaching the Gospel that the Kingdom of God was about to come. . . . Our apostles also knew, through Our Lord Jesus Christ, that there would be strife on the question of the bishop's office. Therefore, for this reason, since they had complete foreknowledge, they appointed the aforesaid persons and later made further provisions that if they should fall asleep, other tested men should succeed in their ministry.[4]

Likewise, Irenaeus, in his treatise *Against Heresies*, maintained that the apostles had "perfect knowledge" and maintained that they appointed bishops to whom they passed on their sacred "mysteries."[5]

Since the apostles were therefore designated by Jesus as His representatives and as the repository of sacred truth, and since the New Testament comes from their pen and that of their immediate associates, it is a good thing to examine in detail what can be known about these most eminent of men. In recounting the lives of the "inner circle" of apostles (Peter, James and John, as well as Thomas), we have a number of concrete facts. When, on the other hand, we approach the biographies of some of the more obscure apostles (such as James, the son of Alphaeus, Simon Kananaios, Jude Thaddaeus and especially Matthias, who replaced Judas Iscariot) the best we can say is "perhaps," and we are forced to admit that most of what we can say derives from the realm of folklore. Even so, it is not unimportant to know what Christians fairly close in time to them believed.

10

1

Simon bar Jonah: The little fisherman

IT is appropriate that we begin our study with the life of the "rock" upon whom Christ founded His Church. St. Peter, the Prince of Apostles, with the help of the Holy Spirit, united 120 confused, dispirited followers of Jesus and, within days, built a Church numbering more than 5,000 souls. Many skeptics dismiss or denigrate St. Peter as a weak, bumbling vacillator, insisting that it was St. Paul who built the Church *in spite of* St. Peter. No one who reads the Acts of the Apostles, however, can fail to see that Peter's role in Christ's Church was equal to that of his friend Paul.

What do we know of the life of St. Peter, who is always first in the lists of the apostles provided by the evangelists? What did he look like? Lloyd Douglas, the Lutheran priest and novelist, called him "The Big Fisherman." However, according to archaeologists who studied the bones that Pope Paul VI declared in 1968 to be those of his earliest predecessor, Peter was not big at all: he was a stocky, muscular man, but short — only five feet, four inches tall.[1] Most early representations of him show a fair complexion, curly hair and a short, curly beard. The Vatican archaeologists who examined his relics stated that the bones were those of a man between sixty-seven and seventy-two years of age. Assuming the year of Peter's death as A.D. 67, we arrive at an approximate year of birth between

11

1 and 6 B.C. This would have made him about the same age as Jesus, who was probably born in 6 or 7 B.C. Peter was born on the banks of the Jordan River, almost at the point where it empties into the Sea of Galilee, in a little town called Bethsaida. According to most scholars, the name of the town meant "fisherman's haven." It is likely that Bethsaida was just that, a tiny village inhabited chiefly by families who made their living fishing on the big lake.

Peter's given name was Simon and his father's name was John (or Jonah, a variant spelling). In later life he would sign his name "Simon bar Jonah." Many Jews of that time did not have surnames that were handed down from generation to generation. They were identified by a given name followed by a patronymic (as in the case of Peter) or their place of birth (as in Jesus of Nazareth). Peter's mother was allegedly named Joanna, but we have no idea how many children were in the family besides the brother Andrew, apparently somewhat younger, who also became an apostle. Since Bethsaida was in a part of Palestine that had a large gentile, or pagan, population, young Simon almost certainly learned Greek as well as the native dialect Aramaic.

Although education was not made compulsory for all children in Palestine until A.D. 64, the traditional teachings of the rabbis forbade pious Jews to live in any town without a school. We can say, almost with certainty, that at age six, young Simon was sent to school, which was held, no doubt, at the local synagogue. Like the Puritans of seventeenth-century New England, the Jews of the first century were mainly interested in teaching their children so that they could read the Scriptures. After being taught his letters, for the next seven years Simon was taught the Scriptures by rote. He was taught little, if any, mathematics, history, science or geography. If Simon had sisters, it is uncertain whether they participated with him in schooling. Most rabbis of the time discouraged the education of girls. One of them declared, "It would be better to see the Torah burnt than hear its words upon the lips of women."[2] Some girls, however, did go to school. It is clear, when one reads the first chapter of St. Luke, that Our Lady did know the Torah, and was not ashamed to have its words on her lips. She, no doubt, had been educated, and there were other Jewish girls who were given the same advantage.

Simon's formal education probably came to an end when he was about thirteen. Other boys who were destined for theological studies went further. Men who had completed a full course of such studies were generally considered "learned." It was for this reason that most of the scholars of Peter's day looked down on him and the other apostles as "unlearned, ignorant men." It is not that they were unable to read or write, but they did not have extensive theological training. Therefore, to the minds of the scholars, the apostles had no right to instruct others in spiritual things.

As a teenager, then, Simon bar Jonah probably went to work as a fisherman. The Sea of Galilee was very rich in fish, with twenty-six varieties noted at the time. According to French historian Henri Daniel-Rops, the fishermen of the time used hooks made of copper, brass or iron, and two kinds of nets. The first was a throwing net, round and about twelve feet across, with leads around the edge, designed to catch fish by dropping over them. The second was known as the *sagene* and was a band about 1,500 feet long and twelve feet deep, with floaters above and sinkers below. This was the dragnet to which Jesus referred to when He said, "The reign of God is also like a dragnet thrown into the lake, which collected all sorts of things. When it was full they hauled it ashore and sat down to put what was worthwhile into containers. What was useless they threw away." (Mt. 13:47-48) Fishermen used wide, solid boats which usually held a crew of six or eight, with one man as captain. The owners of the fishing boats on the Sea of Galilee are believed to have belonged to a guild. Through this they sold their fish to the wholesalers of Jerusalem for a good price and the proceeds were usually shared by the owners with the hired men.

Probably when Simon was in his late teens or early twenties, his father chose a bride for him. Almost all Jews of that time, except those who were members of the ascetic Essene community, married. Many of the rabbis considered that a bachelor was not even a man in the full sense. Almost all marriages were arranged with near relatives, often first cousins. Although Peter appears to have been married for more than fifty years, we know next to nothing about his wife. Some early Church Fathers asserted that her name was Perpetua. This was a Roman name, and, unless Peter married a Roman girl, it is unlikely that Perpetua was the name that she bore from birth (if indeed she ever bore it). Later in life, when she and her husband worked extensively among Greeks and Romans, she may have chosen to take that name.

We do not know how many children resulted from that union, although the *Acts of Peter* mentions a daughter, sometimes called Petronilla, who was born after the Resurrection of Christ and was permanently crippled by sickness at the age of ten. Nevertheless, she is supposed to have survived the martyrdom of her parents to live until A.D. 98, when she was in her sixties. Some archaeologists have uncovered a first-century tombstone in Rome with an inscription that seems to corroborate the fact that one Petronilla, a daughter of Peter, died in that year. There are no references to any other children, and if there were, they may have died young.

In A.D. 28 Simon bar Jonah, then in his early thirties,

lived with his wife and her family in the town of Capernaum on the north shore of the Sea of Galilee, west of the Jordan River. He was now the proprietor of a boat, and, along with his younger brother Andrew, worked in partnership with another boat owner, Zebedee, whose sons James and John were Peter's age and his close friends. Galilean fishermen had the reputation of being the most pious of Jews, and Simon and Andrew were no exception. Peter, from boyhood up, was a strict observer of the Jewish law. Later, he would affirm that in all his life nothing "unclean" (that is, forbidden by the Jewish dietary regulations) had ever touched his lips. Both Peter and Andrew, as well as the sons of Zebedee, were evidently disciples of the prophet known to history as John the Baptist, so called because of his practice of immersing his followers in the Jordan.

One day Andrew came to Simon in a state of great excitement. "We have found the Messiah!" Immediately Simon dropped what he was doing and went with his brother to meet the man whom John the Baptist had identified as "God's Chosen One." We are not told specifically where the meeting took place, but, from St. John's Gospel, we are led to believe that it occurred in Bethany — properly Bethabara, instead of a town in the Jordan Valley some sixteen miles east of Jerusalem and its suburb of Bethany (which was the home of Mary, Martha and Lazarus).

As soon as Simon was introduced to the Messiah, whose name was Jesus of Nazareth, the Lord said, "You are Simon, son of John; Your name shall be Cephas (which is rendered Peter)." (Jn. 1:42) The word "Cephas" is a Greek *transliteration* of an Aramaic word which means "rock." "Petros," from which we get the English "Peter," is a *translation*. Among Jews, Peter was doubtless called Cephas, or *Kefos*, and among gentiles, Petros. This was Simon's surname. In those days the last name was frequently not inherited, but given when its bearer was an adult. It usually told something about the person who bore it, whether it was his occupation, physical appearance or his personality. Our Lord named Simon "Peter" because the name evidently reflected his personality.

Simon Peter returned to Galilee with the Lord. He and Andrew did not at once become His constant companions, but continued, for a time, in the fishing business.

Some weeks or months later, probably sometime in A.D. 29, John the Baptist was arrested. He had dared to denounce the local ruler, or *tetrarch,* of Galilee, Herod Antipas. Herod had divorced his wife to marry the wife of his half-brother, Philip, and John had sharply criticized this breach of the marital bond. John would eventually be murdered to satisfy a whim of Salome, the daughter of the tetrarch's new wife. Shortly after John's arrest, Simon encountered Jesus again. Simon and Andrew were in their boat one morning along the shore of the Sea of Galilee, cleaning their nets. They had caught absolutely nothing. A large crowd gathered as Jesus spoke, and grew so numerous that the Lord commandeered Peter's boat and sat preaching from its rostrum.

If Simon Peter was taken aback at Jesus' sudden appropriation of his boat, he was even more shocked when He told him to "put out into deep water and lower your nets for a catch." Peter replied, "Master, we have been hard at it all night long and have caught nothing; but if you say so, I will lower the nets." (Lk. 5:5)

Many a fisherman might have resented Jesus' command. Simon Peter had been fishing on the Sea of Galilee for twenty years, and he was perfectly convinced that conditions were not right that day for a significant catch.

However, even after only two meetings, Peter seemed to know that Jesus was more than just a learned rabbi.

Peter did as he was bidden. He and his employees prepared the appropriate nets and moved into deep water. The nets were lowered and instantly they enclosed so immense a school of fish that they began to split. The men had to signal to their partners in the other boat to come to their assistance. When men, fish and boats were safely on shore again, Peter ran up to Jesus, fell at His feet and cried, "Leave me, Lord. I am a sinful man." (Lk. 5:8)

One of Peter's most striking qualities was his love for Jesus and his unconditional loyalty. A deeply pious Jew, Peter realized that he was in the presence of a higher being and felt totally inadequate. Simon Peter at once understood that, devout man though he was, he was unworthy to stand in the presence of the man he recognized as Israel's Messiah.

In fact, Peter's awe and that of his companions James and John was so immense that it bordered on fear. They knew the sea well enough to know that there was no natural explanation for their extraordinary catch. The Lord, however, put Peter and his two friends at ease. "Do not be afraid. From now on you will be catching men." (Lk. 5:10) The spectacular catch of fish was granted by Jesus as a sign of their true calling. Just as they had caught the miraculous draught of fish through His power, through the same grace they would draw men into the kingdom of God. As soon as they moored their boats on shore, the three fishermen left the fishing business forever to follow their Master. They had all been members of the middle class and had a fairly prosperous business. Yet, as Peter later said, "We have left everything to follow You."

Many have wondered why most of the disciples that Jesus chose were "poor fishermen" and not learned theologians. It is clear that Jesus was searching for pious men without religious preconceptions. Men with a formal theological education, who considered themselves experts, tended to be resentful of ideas other than their own. St.

Paul, for example, had been a learned theologian, who throughout Christ's stay on earth was disdainful of Him and His teachings. The fishermen of Galilee, although capable and intelligent, were not "experts" liable to claim to know more about the Messiah than the Messiah knew about himself. On the contrary, they were open and teachable.

Almost immediately after the draught of fish, Jesus went to a synagogue in Capernaum. There He was confronted by a man "with an unclean spirit" who shrieked, "What do you want of us, Jesus of Nazareth? Have you come to destroy us? I know who you are — the holy One of God!" (Mk. 1:24) When Jesus declared, "Be quiet! Come out of the man!" — the man was cured. The event created a sensation in the town.

After Jesus had spoken in the synagogue, He went with James and John to the house where Peter and Perpetua lived with her mother. Andrew, who was apparently unmarried, lived there too. When Peter and Andrew arrived with their guests, they found the matriarch in bed with a high fever. There was no way that these men could possibly be accommodated for the evening, even if one of them *was* the Messiah, Perpetua doubtless explained. At this point Jesus asked to see Perpetua's mother. Going to her bedside, he commanded the fever to leave her. Instantly healed, Peter's mother-in-law was able to leave her bed to accommodate her guests.

Thereafter, Peter's house in Capernaum became Jesus' headquarters. Whenever He was there, the evangelists spoke of His being "at home." The very night of His first stay there, the house was deluged by crowds of sick and afflicted. St. Mark recorded that "they brought him all who were ill, and those possessed by demons. Before long the whole town was gathered outside the door." (Mk. 1:32-33)

Surely Peter's wife and mother-in-law are two unsung heroines of the Bible. It took a great level of commitment for these ladies, one of whom may have had young children, to permit their home to be the headquarters for the ministry of a man, who, however much of His identity they may have understood, was nevertheless the center of controversy. From then on their lives were never the same. Their home became a hotel, an auditorium and a hospital, visited not only by people with all sorts of diseases, but also by individuals made violent and blasphemous by the indwelling of demons. Truly, Perpetua and her mother must have been courageous women, loyal not only to Peter but to Jesus as well. Their hospitality was certainly strained to the limit some days later when Jesus returned from preaching in neighboring villages, and, once again, the house was surrounded by a sea of people. This was the occasion when four men, carrying their crippled friend on a stretcher, unable to get near the door because of the immense crowd, hauled their invalid to the top of the roof and knocked a hole in it in order to lower their afflicted companion into the presence of Jesus, there to be forgiven and healed. It must have been a great trial for Peter's womenfolk.

It was probably at this time that Jesus formally called His Twelve Apostles. From the beginning, it was clear that Peter was their leader. He was the most outspoken, the most inquisitive, the most courageous, even if heart occasionally came before head. It was Peter who was the first to acknowledge Jesus as Messiah and Son of God. This occurred when Jesus and His disciples were visiting the city of Caesarea Philippi. Just north of Galilee, it was the capital of the dominion of Herod Philip. Somewhere outside the city, amidst the tall rocky cliffs, Jesus asked His disciples, "Who do people say that the Son of Man is?" Most of the apostles hedged. "Some say John the Baptizer,

19

others Elijah, still others Jeremiah or one of the prophets." "And you," he said to them, "who do you say that I am?" "You are the Messiah," Simon Peter answered, "the Son of the living God!" (Mt. 16:16)

Jesus replied, "Blest are you, Simon son of Jonah! No mere man has revealed this to you, but my heavenly Father. I for my part declare to you, you are 'Rock,' and on this rock I will build my Church, and the jaws of death shall not prevail against it. I will entrust to you the keys of the kingdom of heaven. Whatever you declare bound on earth shall be bound in heaven; whatever you declare loosed on earth shall be loosed in heaven." (Mt. 16:17-19) These words, besides providing the image of Peter as the doorkeeper of the pearly gates, sparked much controversy over the years. It is perfectly clear that Jesus named Peter the chief of the apostolic college. It is also perfectly clear that Jesus proclaimed that it was to be through Peter that His eternal Church would be established on earth. It is moreover a fact that Jesus authorized Peter to act as His regent on earth in the matter of Church laws and discipline. At all times, the Christian is to look to the Church rather than to private insights or inspiration as the source of truth.

After the conversation at Caesarea Philippi, it was evident that Peter's primacy among the Twelve did not mean that he was above his Master's rebuke. After Peter had acknowledged Jesus as the Son of God, the Lord indicated "that he [Jesus] must go to Jerusalem and suffer greatly there at the hands of the elders, the chief priests, and the scribes, and to be put to death, and raised up on the third day." (Mt. 16:21) Peter was horrified and insisted that he would never permit such a thing to happen. He must have been surprised when Jesus, far from pleased by his pledge of loyalty, seemed to turn on him, saying, "Get out of my sight, you satan! You are trying to make me trip and fall. You are not judging by God's standards but by man's." (Mt. 16:23) None of the apostles were able to reconcile themselves with the idea of a suffering Messiah or to realize that, in their intentions to save His life, they were actually trying to hinder God's will.

Most Jews thought of the Messiah as a glorious king who would achieve fame and glory in the world, culminating His ministry by driving out the Romans and setting up an earthly government where peace, justice and prosperity endured. Peter, too, had similar expectations. He recognized Jesus as the Messiah, but expected Him to proceed to inaugurate a glorious kingdom in which he himself, as the Messiah's right-hand man, could expect fame, riches and glory. He was therefore bewildered and horrified when Jesus talked darkly of suffering, rejection and death. This was impossible! That would defeat everything all religious Jews had ever longed for! It must not be permitted to happen!

After Jesus made it clear that this *had* to happen, He and the Twelve left Caesarea Philippi to make the thirty-mile journey on foot to a mountain near Jesus' hometown of Nazareth, a mountain known as Tabor. The journey took six days. As they traveled they preached and healed in all the villages throughout Israel, and, when not ministering, the Lord instructed the Twelve and other disciples. It was a sort of moving seminary in which the apostles learned not only by word but by deed.

What happened on Mount Tabor was one of the most moving events in Peter's life. St. Mark tells us that "Jesus took Peter, James, and John off by themselves with him and led them up a high mountain. He was transfigured before their eyes and his clothes became dazzlingly white — whiter than the work of any bleacher could make them. Elijah appeared to them along with Moses; the two were in conversation with Jesus." (Mk. 9:2-4)

21

Peter, as usual, was the first to speak, although he did not know what to say. "Rabbi, how good it is for us to be here! Let us erect three booths on this site, one for you, one for Moses, and one for Elijah." (Mk. 9:5) He somehow wanted to preserve the experience by building shrines on the sight of the appearances, a feeble human way of trying to grasp the significance of an event beyond normal human experience. Before Peter could say more, "A cloud came, overshadowing them, and out of the cloud a voice: 'This is my Son, my beloved. Listen to him.' Suddenly, looking around, they no longer saw anyone with them — only Jesus." (Mk. 9:7-8)

Of this experience St. Peter would many years later write:

It was not by way of cleverly concocted myths that we taught you about the coming in power of our Lord Jesus Christ, for we were eyewitnesses of his sovereign majesty. He received glory and praise from God the Father when that unique declaration came to him out of the majestic splendor: 'This is my beloved Son, on whom my favor rests.' We ourselves heard this said from heaven while we were in his company on the holy mountain. Besides, we possess the prophetic message as something altogether reliable. Keep your attention closely fixed on it, as you would on a lamp shining in a dark place until the first streaks of dawn appear and the morning star rises in your hearts. (II Pt. 1:16-19)

Peter here makes clear the significance of the Transfiguration to him. He had been confused and dismayed by Jesus' talk of suffering and death. Perhaps he had even begun to entertain involuntary doubts that his Master was really the Messiah. The Transfiguration cleared away all his doubts. When he saw the greatest prophets of the Old

Testament worshiping the glorified Jesus, Peter realized that all prophecy spoke of Jesus and His destiny to suffer and die. Peter also realized that human understanding is like a "dark place" that needs to be illumined by the lamp of God's Word. Nevertheless, there continued to be times when Peter did not understand, even in light of the most stupendous display of divine grace.

The incident in which Peter walked on water is well-known. This may have occurred before the events at Caesarea Philippi and the Transfiguration, but it is not certain. Jesus, having multiplied bread and fish enough to satisfy a crowd of more than 15,000, went off by himself to pray. He bade the Twelve cross by boat to the other side of the Sea of Galilee. In the wee hours of the morning, when the apostles' boat was far out on the lake and they were battling against a strong headwind and rough sea, they saw a figure approaching them, walking on the surface of the lake. Terrified, they thought they were seeing a ghost. St. Matthew recorded that they were literally screaming with fear when they heard Jesus' voice, "Get hold of yourselves! It is I. Do not be afraid!" (Mt. 14:27)

Peter still was not completely convinced that he was not being toyed with by some malign spirit and said, "Lord, if it is really you, tell me to come to you across the water." The answer came, "Come!" (Mt. 14:28)

Why did Peter do this? Did he think that this was a skill that could be taught? Did he want to prove to himself that Jesus was really walking on *water* and not, as some interpreters have suggested, on rocks and sandbars? No, Peter wanted to walk on water as an act of faith. He knew that if it was really Jesus who was speaking to them, no harm would befall him. If what they saw was a demon or ghost, he would drown. So he put his life on the line as an act of faith. He stepped out of the boat into the water. As long as Peter's faith was fixed on the Lord, he walked on the water. But when his attention slipped to his own weakness and the hostility of the elements, he began to sink. Doubtless Peter told of this event in later years to illustrate the fact that we must put our faith not in our own ability or preparations, but in the Lord's grace, and that we can triumph over the most impossible circumstances if Christ assists us.

Peter, of course, figured prominently in the Passion of the Lord. Jesus sent him, along with John, to prepare the room that He had engaged for the Passover meal that has come to be called the Last Supper. The Passover was, of course, the most important of the Jewish festivals. It commemorates the passing over of the Angel of Death, which spared the children of Israel when it struck down the firstborn of the Egyptians at the time of the Exodus.

Whenever a Jew entered a house in those days, he removed his shoes and placed his feet over a copper bowl. They were then usually washed by a servant, who poured water over them, rubbed them with his hands, and wiped them with a towel. When there was no servant, the host performed the office, but Peter was aghast that Jesus himself would stoop to perform so menial a task. "I will never let You wash my feet," he protested. Jesus insisted on performing the office in order to demonstrate that no Christian should ever consider himself too good or too important to perform a useful service for another human being, no matter how menial the service may seem. When Peter realized that this disturbing situation was not simply a result of an oversight on the part of his colleagues but Jesus' deliberate choice, he insisted that Jesus wash his entire body, so greatly did he desire to please his Master. Peter, the man of humility and obedience, often expressed himself in what would appear to be a childish and simple way. However, no one can deny that he yearned with all his being to serve and please his Lord.

24

It was at this feast that Jesus declared, "Your faith in me shall be shaken, for Scripture has it, 'I will strike the shepherd and the sheep will be dispersed.' " (Mk. 14:27) Peter protested, "Even though all are shaken in faith, it will not be that way with me." (Mk. 14:29) Jesus told him, "I give you my assurance, this very night before the cock crows twice, you will deny me three times." Peter still argued, "Even if I have to die with you, I will not deny you." (Mk. 14:30-31)

Luke wrote that Jesus continued, saying, "Simon, Simon. Remember that Satan has asked for you, to sift you all like wheat. But I have prayed for you that your faith may never fail. You in turn must strengthen your brothers." (Lk. 22:31-32) Although Peter continued to insist that he was ready to go with Him to prison and to death, the Lord insisted that he would deny Him thrice by morning. What can the strongest human will, unaided, avail against the power of Satan?

Jesus took His apostles to a large hill east of the city, known as the Mount of Olives, to pray and meditate. After a while, He took Peter, James and John with Him to a grove known as Gethsemane, where He bade them pray "that you may not be put to the test," warning that "the spirit is willing but nature is weak." (Mk. 14:38) Peter, John and James stayed awake long enough to catch parts of Jesus' spoken prayers, to hear Him pray that His cup might pass from Him, "Father, if it is your will, take this cup from me; yet not my will but yours be done." (Mk. 14:36)

Despite repeated pleas by Jesus, Peter and his companions roused themselves only when a detachment of police arrived. The Jewish authorities, led by Judas Iscariot, arrested Jesus just as if He was a common criminal. In a desperate attempt to fulfill his promise to protect his Lord, Peter, who had been concealing a short sword, lunged at Jesus' attackers and cut off the ear of a servant of the high priest. Jesus healed the man and ordered Peter to disarm. "Those who use the sword are sooner or later destroyed by it. Do you not suppose I can call on my Father to provide at a moment's notice more than twelve legions of angels? But then how would the Scriptures be fulfilled which say it must happen this way?" (Mt. 26:52-54)

Some will argue, from the fact that Peter was willing to lay violent hands upon his Lord's attackers, that the apostle was by nature a rough, ill-tempered man, almost a thug. Does this incident illustrate a violent disposition or an overwhelming (if misguided) commitment to his Master? Does it perhaps show a devout, pious man so committed to his Lord that he is ready to act out of character and do bodily violence?

While James apparently followed the other apostles in fleeing for his life in this hour of darkness, Peter and John insisted on following Jesus to the palace of the high priest. Through John, who was apparently a friend of someone in the high priestly family, Peter was admitted with him to the courtyard, where they were able to hear the trial going on within the house. The female servant at the door asked Peter if he was a disciple of the prisoner. "I am not!" he insisted, as he would again when questioned a few minutes later by another woman. When, later in the night, he was identified as a disciple by a third person, Peter, frantic with terror, "broke into curses" and "with an oath" shouted, "I do not even know the man you are talking about!" (Mk. 14:71) No sooner had Peter concluded this pathetic display of cowardice than the cock crowed and the crumbling "rock" rushed from the courtyard sobbing hysterically.

Some have argued that it was not merely out of shameful cowardice that Peter denied his Master. Had

Peter admitted that he was a disciple of Jesus, he would, no doubt, have been compelled to testify before the high priest. The Jewish Supreme Council, or Sanhedrin, was trying to obtain witnesses who would declare that Jesus had claimed to be God — a blasphemy punishable by death. Had Peter been forced to testify, he would have been compelled to give evidence that would have brought about his Lord's death. Therefore, Peter must have felt that he was in an impossible situation, in which he could not fail to act disgracefully, no matter what he did. Whatever his motivation, whether fidelity to Jesus or blind panic, Peter was devastated, and we hear nothing more of him until the Lord's Resurrection.

In I Corinthians, St. Paul states that St. Peter was the first apostle to whom the Lord appeared after His Resurrection. He goes into no details. No appearance exclusively to Peter is mentioned by either Matthew or Mark, but Luke records that the apostles reported to the two disciples whom the Lord had met on the way to Emmaus that the Lord had risen and appeared to Simon. (Lk. 24:34) John implies that St. Mary Magdalene was the first person to see the risen Lord. After she told the apostles that the tomb was empty, Peter and John ran to the tomb and ascertained that in fact it was. It was after this that Jesus appeared in person to Mary Magdalene. As the Lord appeared to all the apostles except Thomas that very evening, Peter's personal encounter must have occurred either just before or (more likely) just after the appearance to Mary.

St. John also recounts a Resurrection appearance that is strikingly reminiscent of the time when Jesus bade Peter to leave his fishing nets behind and follow Him. Jesus appeared on the shore of the Sea of Galilee one morning at dawn and shouted to Peter, who along with six other apostles, was fishing, "Children, have you caught anything to eat?" "Not a thing," they answered. "Cast your net off to the starboard side . . . and you will find something." (Jn. 21:5-6)

Indeed, they made such a catch that they could not haul the net in. Peter, who in the earlier incident had told the Lord to leave him because he was a sinful man, this time threw on his clothes (he had stripped) and jumped overboard. After his denial, Peter felt especially unworthy of the presence of his Lord (even though He had appeared personally to him), and, moreover, was embarrassed and ashamed.

The Lord gave Peter three occasions to atone, symbolically at least, for his threefold denial. "Simon, son of John, do you love me more than these?" "Yes, Lord, you know that I love you." "Feed my lambs," Jesus said.

Jesus repeated the question a second and then a third time. Peter, hurt, protested, "Lord, you know everything. You know well that I love you." For the third time, Jesus told him to feed His sheep. (Jn. 21:15-17) Our Lord thus absolved Peter, led him into a reaffirmation of faith and love that confirmed His forgiveness and, at the same time, reaffirmed Peter's leadership over the Christian community.

Jesus' last words to Peter before His Ascension concerned the apostle's eventual death. "I tell you solemnly: as a young man you fastened your belt and went about as you pleased; but when you are older you will stretch out your hands and another will tie you fast and carry you off against your will." (Jn. 21:18) The expression, "to stretch out your hands," means absolutely nothing to us today, but to a person of Peter's time it was a clear reference to crucifixion. Peter was not so otherworldly as to be indifferent to this horrible prospect, and petulantly asked the Lord about the fate of his friend John. "But Lord, what about him?" It is almost as if Peter asked, "Why me? Is it going to happen to the others, too? Or am I the only one who is going to suffer?" Jesus, of course, told Peter that John's fate was none of his concern. Then He levitated from the ground and vanished in a glorious cloud of light. So concluded Peter's dialogues with the Lord in the flesh.

Peter immediately took command of the Christian community. The first part of the Acts of the Apostles is a clear record that Peter was indeed the "rock" upon whom the Church was established. It was Peter who rallied his brethren around him and led them, as a glorious army, into the midst of the hostile inhabitants of Jerusalem, where, within a matter of days, they won such a resounding victory against Satan that more than 5,000 people gave their lives and hearts to Christ.

2

'Upon this rock. . .'

THE Lord, before His Ascension, directed the apostles to remain in Jerusalem until they received the Holy Spirit. Most of them, in fact, were to make their home there for at least a decade. For Peter, living in Jerusalem was quite a change from quiet village life. Cicero called Jerusalem a "hole in the wall." Although there could be no comparison with Rome and Alexandria, with both having well over a million inhabitants, and Antioch, which had nearly as many, Jerusalem, teeming with about 300,000 people crammed into a fairly small area, was extremely busy. It was certainly the largest urban area in which Peter had lived to date. Some considered it ugly. Ringed about with heavily fortified walls, Jerusalem was a town of cramped, zigzagging streets, dark, dirty, and so narrow as to exclude vehicular traffic of any kind. There were few gardens or trees. The streets were jammed, not only with people, but with cattle, sheep and other animals. Foreigners complained of the constant stench of cooking, rubbish (which was burned just outside the city walls) and burnt sacrifices in the temple. Although the rich lived in fine homes, most of the populace, including, no doubt, the apostles, lived in simple cottages roofed with reeds or earth.

The great glory of Jerusalem was the temple. There were scores of synagogues, or houses of prayer. But the temple, where Yahweh, the God of Abraham, Isaac and Jacob dwelt, was the center of Jewish worship. This magnificent edifice, rebuilt only a generation earlier by Herod the Great, was surrounded by various courts and outbuildings. According to the historian Josephus, it was "covered with gold all over." He said that it "had everything that could amaze either mind or eye. Overlaid all around with stout plates of gold, in the first rays of the sun it reflected so fierce a blaze of fire that those who endeavored to look at it were forced to turn away, as if they had looked into the sun. To strangers as they approached, it seemed in the distance like a mountain covered with snow; for any part not covered with gold was dazzlingly white."[1]

It was in the upper story of a house near the temple that the Twelve met for some days after the Ascension to devote themselves to prayer. One wonders how large a house it was, for St. Luke recorded that not only the Twelve met there, but also Our Lady and several female disciples (which probably included Mary Magdalene, Mary and Martha and the mothers of James and John and James, the son of Alphaeus). Even though people in those days tended to live in incredibly crowded quarters (by contemporary American standards), it is likely that not everyone who prayed in the upper room stayed there. It was at a meeting here, incidentally, that Peter insisted on filling the vacancy created in the apostolic college by the defection of Judas Iscariot.

It is generally assumed that the first Christians were meeting in the upper room on Pentecost, but this is impossible. Luke simply says that on the day of Pentecost the Church was "together in one place." He speaks of a sound from heaven filling the whole house (*oikos*), but this word could be used loosely for "place" or "hall." Inasmuch as the disciples could be heard and observed by large crowds of people, it is likely that they were in a public meeting place. We know that for some years afterward the Church met at a place known as Solomon's Portico, on the grounds of the temple, and it is likely that they were meeting here on Pentecost. Solomon's Portico was one of several colonnades that surrounded the temple. The pillars were thirty-seven feet tall and made of white marble, and the ceiling was paneled with cedar. The portico was forty-five feet wide. Thus it was a large area, closed to the sky but mostly exposed on the sides, fairly wide and well over a hundred feet long.

It was on the day of Pentecost, the festival in which the Jews celebrated the giving of the law to Moses, when "suddenly from up in the sky there came a noise like a strong, driving wind which was heard all through the house where they were seated. Tongues as of fire appeared, which parted and came to rest on each of them. All were filled with the Holy Spirit. They began to express themselves in foreign tongues and made bold proclamation as the Spirit prompted them." (Acts 2:2-4)

Most ancient commentators interpret the "gift of tongues" as the ability to speak, without preparation, in foreign languages, while most modern interpreters feel that what was involved was the "language of ecstasy" common in today's "charismatic" meetings. However the phenomenon of the Baptism of the Spirit and the "gift of tongues" are explained, the meeting on the day of Pentecost was noisy enough to attract the attention of a huge crowd of temple worshipers. These people included individuals from all parts of the Mediterranean, all of whom heard the apostles and their company extolling the greatness of God. Each of the foreigners heard God's praises in his own language. Some were thunderstruck. Others tried to make light of the situation by accusing the apostles of being drunk. This provided Peter with the opportunity to give what has been called the first Christian sermon. Indeed, a noted modern preacher said that Peter's greatest quality was his boldness: his willingness to take risks, to put himself on the line. Pentecost was an example of this. His Master had less than two months before been killed for telling the world who He was. Peter knew that he ran the risk of being instantly mobbed and killed by the same people whose hands were still stained, figuratively, with the blood of his Lord. Yet he spoke.

He began by refuting the accusation that the worshipers were drunk. Then he quoted the prophet Joel, declaring, in God's name:

In the last days, says God, . . .I will pour out a portion of my spirit on all mankind: Your sons and daughters shall prophesy, your young men shall see visions and your old men shall dream dreams. Yes, even on my servants and handmaids I will pour out a portion of my spirit in those days, and they shall prophesy. I will work wonders in the heavens above and signs on the earth below: blood, fire, and a cloud of smoke. The sun shall be turned to darkness and the moon to blood before the coming of that great and glorious day of the Lord. Then everyone shall be saved who calls on the name of the Lord. (Acts 2:17-21)

After quoting Joel, Peter spoke of Jesus, who fulfilled the words of prophecy "with miracles, wonders, and signs as his credentials. These God worked through him in your midst, as you well know." (Acts 2:22)

Everyone in Jerusalem knew about Jesus and His ministry. Most people, however, were in a state of confusion, even fear over His Crucifixion and the reports of His Resurrection. Peter addressed their perplexity about Jesus, frankly telling his Jewish hearers that it was they who had killed Him and God who raised Him. "He was delivered up by the set purpose and plan of God; you even made use of pagans to crucify and kill him. God freed him from death's bitter pangs, however, and raised him up again, for it was impossible that death should keep its hold on him." (Acts 2:23-24)

Once again Peter quoted Scripture foretelling Christ's Resurrection. He concluded by declaring, "Let the whole house of Israel know beyond any doubt that God has made both Lord and Messiah this Jesus whom you crucified." (Acts 2:36) Peter had good reason to fear that the crowd would go wild with rage and surge forward to lynch him and his colleagues. But such was not the case. Convinced and convicted, the people were "deeply shaken," and asked, "What are we to do, brothers?"

"You must reform and be baptized, each one of you, in the name of Jesus Christ, that your sins may be forgiven; then you will receive the gift of the Holy Spirit," said Peter. Three thousand people were baptized and experienced the "Baptism of the Spirit," which they had derided only moments before.

Luke recorded that from the start, Peter's ministry, empowered from on high, was accompanied by miracles. It was the complete cure of a well-known beggar at the temple that brought the Church to the attention of the Jewish authorities. Later, in the town of Lydda, Peter healed a paralyzed man named Aeneas. A few days later, in the nearby town of Joppa, he raised from the dead a woman named Tabitha. Perhaps the event that impressed people most strikingly was the strange death of a couple named Ananias and Sapphira. It was common for converts to sell all their assets and give the proceeds to the apostles to be distributed equally, according to need, among the entire brotherhood. This couple, after selling some property, donated some to the apostles, but secretly held back the rest for their own use. When Peter, through supernatural enlightenment, announced to Ananias and later to Sapphira that they had lied to the Holy Spirit, both of them, in turn, crumpled to the floor, dead at Peter's feet. One need not assume that Peter used his spiritual gifts maliciously to put a "whammy" or an "evil eye" on the unfortunate couple. The miracle here was supernatural intuition. Neither Peter nor the other apostles had anything to do directly with their death. If we were to assume that Ananias and Sapphira had just undergone an overwhelming experience of the immediacy of God, the remorse following their conviction of sin may very well have been so devastating as literally to stop their hearts. As a result of this and numerous other miracles, people kept gathering at Solomon's porch and even "carried the sick into the streets and laid them on cots and mattresses, so that when Peter passed by at least his shadow might fall on one or another of them. Crowds from the towns around Jerusalem would gather, too, bringing their sick and those who were troubled by unclean spirits, all of whom were cured." (Acts 5:15-16).

Events of this sort attracted the attention of the Jewish authorities. It was the healing of the cripple at the "Beautiful Gate" of the temple that caused the first arrests of Christians. After Peter and John used the healing as an opportunity to invite the crowds that had been attracted by the miracles to repent, the two apostles were clapped in jail. The next day they had a hearing before the Sanhedrin.

The Sanhedrin was a council of seventy-one men who were a sort of state government within the Roman Empire. Somewhat like a modern local government, they administered civil and criminal law with the extent of their power defined by Rome and subject to Rome. Since Israel was traditionally a theocracy, with no distinction between religious law and secular law, the Sanhedrin had complete control over Jewish religious affairs. It was composed of the chief priests, the elders, and the scribes, mentioned so often in the Bible. The chief priests were members of the high priestly family. The elders were the heads of the major Israelitic clans. The scribes were ecclesiastical lawyers, specialists on interpreting not only the regulations from what we call the Old Testament, but also from the huge body of oral teaching that had arisen in more recent centuries. Most of the scribes belonged to the sect of Pharisees, who were passionate in their concern to observe the law with scrupulous exactitude. They frequently clashed with the priests and elders, many of whom were of the Sadducee sect, who disclaimed any belief in a world to come, and insisted that man has no soul and this life is all there is.

Of course, the Sanhedrin could put no one to death without the approval of Rome, in the person of the governor. From A.D. 26 to 36 the governor of Judea was Pontius Pilate, who had tried halfheartedly to save Jesus from being crucified, and whose wife, Claudia Procula, may have been a Christian or at least sympathetic to Christianity.

The cards were not entirely stacked against Peter and John when they were hauled before the Sanhedrin. The seventy-one members of the council were not united in lockstep. While the Sadducees could be counted on to be unremittingly hostile, the Pharisees tended to be less so. We must not forget that there were at least two Christians on the Sanhedrin: Joseph of Arimathea and Nicodemus. Although this was the same body that had condemned Jesus to death, they still needed to exert pressure on the Roman governor to carry out the sentence.

Peter, John and the former cripple were brought before the Sanhedrin. "By what power or in whose name have men of your stripe done this?" the apostles were asked.

Peter, "filled with the Holy Spirit," answered: "If we must answer today for a good deed done to a cripple and explain how he was restored to health, then you and all the people of Israel must realize that it was done in the name of Jesus Christ the Nazorean whom you crucified and whom God raised from the dead. In the power of that name this man stands before you perfectly sound. This Jesus is 'the stone rejected by you the builders which has become the cornerstone.' There is salvation in no other name in the whole world given to men by which we are to be saved." (Acts 4:7, 9-12)

Note Peter's amazing boldness. He and John were the prisoners of a legislative body whose murderous tendencies were only too well-known to them. Peter made no attempt at conciliation. He boldly and bald-facedly "tells them like it is." He tells them, in effect, that they are guilty of murdering the Messiah. The act about which they are being questioned has been performed through the man whom they rejected and killed, a man who is the only means of salvation for the entire human race.

The Sanhedrin was taken aback by such boldness, especially on the part of a small businessman who had no theological preparation. In fact, they were "amazed," and when they saw the man who had been cured standing there with them, they were at a loss for words and overwhelmed by a sense of helplessness. "What shall we do with these men?" they asked themselves. "Everyone who lives in Jerusalem knows what a remarkable show of power took place through them. We cannot deny it." Finally they decided simply to warn Peter and John not to repeat the offense. So they dismissed the apostles and told them under no circumstances were they "to mention [Jesus'] name to anyone again." (Acts 4:13-17)

Peter and John in effect told the Sanhedrin, "We can't promise that." Actually they said, "Judge for yourselves whether it is right in God's sight for us to obey you rather than God. Surely we cannot help speaking of what we have seen and heard." (Acts 4:19-20) Even so, the Sanhedrin let them go.

The apostles, of course, continued their ministry, the followers of Jesus continued to multiply and reports of healings increased. This time the Sanhedrin arrested all of the Twelve and threw them into jail. The next day they were astounded to find that they were once again teaching the masses at Solomon's Portico. The apostles told them that "an angel of the Lord" had opened the gates of the jail and told them, "Go out now and take your place in the temple precincts and preach to the people all about this new life." (Acts 5:19,20)

They were rearrested and brought before the Sanhedrin, where the high priest charged them with ignoring their previous order. Peter once again boldly said, "Better for us to obey God than men! The God of our fathers has raised up Jesus whom you put to death, hanging him on a tree. He whom God has exalted at his right hand as ruler and savior is to bring repentance to Israel and forgiveness of sins. We testify to this. So too does the Holy Spirit whom God has given to those that obey him." (Acts 5:29-32)

The high priest and his colleagues were furious and ready to hand the Twelve over to Pilate to be crucified, when a Pharisee named Gamaliel rose to address his brethren. Gamaliel was perhaps the most renowned and respected member of the Sanhedrin, and Israel's foremost theologian at the time. He had the Twelve ordered out of court and then bade his brethren:

Think twice about what you are going to do with these men. Not long ago a certain Theudas came on the scene and tried to pass himself off as someone of importance. About four hundred men joined him. However, he was killed, and all those who had been so easily convinced by him were disbanded. . . . Next came Judas the Galilean at the time of the census. He too built up quite a following, but likewise died, and all his followers were dispersed. The present case is similar. My advice is that you have nothing to do with these men. Let them alone. If their purpose or activity is human in its origins, it will destroy itself. If, on the other hand, it comes from God, you will not be able to destroy them without fighting God himself. (Acts 5:35-39)

Convinced by Gamaliel not to request Pilate to execute the Twelve, the Sanhedrin was content merely to have them tied to a pillar and flogged. They were beaten with a bone- or metal-tipped whip — officially for thirty-nine lashes, but more likely until the guards, who were doing the dirty work, grew tired. When Peter and his brethren staggered home bruised and bloody, they were not filled with bitterness and hatred. They did not mumble to each other about the injustice of "the system." Instead, they were "full of joy that they had been judged worthy of ill-treatment for the sake of the Name." (Acts 5:41) Immediately they returned to Solomon's Portico, where they preached and taught daily.

The Twelve remained in Jerusalem, supervising the Church there and the communities that were springing up through the Middle East. Peter and others made trips to the new communities of "Nazarenes" to baptize, preach, lay on hands and perform whatever functions were necessary.

Very early there appeared two important divisions in the Church founded by Christ; they consisted of the Jewish Christians and the "Hellenists." The Jewish Christians were led by James the Righteous and included many of Jesus' relatives. James felt that it was important for Christians to observe the Law of Moses in its entirety. The Jewish Christians were very numerous in Jerusalem and its environs. Many of the Hellenists, who included perhaps the majority of Christians outside the Jerusalem area, had been pagans who had converted to Judaism and tended to be less strict than the Jewish Christians about keeping the Law of Moses. At any rate, there were some misunderstandings, and the Hellenists began to complain that their widows were not getting as much financial support as the widows among the Jewish Christians. Peter and the Twelve had to mediate and ease whatever hard feelings had arisen.

After this, Peter called the Twelve together and pointed out that it would be a mistake for them to devote so much time to the business of the Church that they had no time to preach and teach. Thus, they selected "seven men acknowledged to be deeply spiritual and prudent" to serve as "deacons." These men were presented by the Twelve to the other Church leaders, and with them prayed and laid hands on them and ordained them to their ministry.

The deacons quickly assumed functions other than administration. Several of them preached extensively. One of these great preachers, St. Stephen, became the first Christian martyr in A.D. 36. He was stoned to death by a mob in Jerusalem with the tacit support of the Jewish authorities, incuding Paul, who witnessed the bloody deed without protest.

Stephen's death led to the conversion of many gentiles, or pagans. Until A.D. 36, all converts, both Judaists and Hellenists, had been Jews. Now, as many of the Hellenists left Jerusalem after the martyrdom of Stephen, they settled in other parts of the Middle East, notably in the cities of Antioch and Damascus, where they made converts from the ranks of the pagans.

Many Christians, especially of the Jerusalem, Judeo-Christian denomination, were disturbed at the admission of gentiles to the Church. They assumed that Christ's revelation was to Jews alone. Scripture stated that the Israelites were God's chosen people. The typical Jewish Christian assumed, correctly, that Jesus was God's final and definitive revelation, the culmination and fulfillment of Judaism. However, the same Jewish Christian also entertained the incorrect assumption that Israel was to remain confined to the descendants of Abraham and Sarah. Peter seemed to have been undecided about this question until he was granted a divine revelation.

In Caesarea, about sixty miles northwest of Jerusalem on the Mediterranean coast, a city where large numbers of Roman troops were garrisoned, there lived a high-ranking army officer named Cornelius. Along with his family, he was sympathetic to the new faith. At 3 P.M. one afternoon Cornelius had a bodily vision of an angel in his home. Terrified, he was put at ease when the celestial being told him, "Your prayer has been heard and your generosity remembered in God's presence." (Acts 10:31) The officer was directed to send for Peter at Joppa, where he was staying with a man named Simon Tanner. Immediately Cornelius sent two slaves and a soldier to the house of the leather tanner.

Joppa was forty miles south of Caesarea on the coast, a full day's journey. At noon the next day Peter was sitting on the roof of the tanner's house, waiting for dinner and using his spare time in the best way possible — by praying. An angel did not appear to him, but he saw something even more unusual:

He saw the sky open and an object come down that looked like a big canvas. It was lowered to the ground by its four corners. Inside it were all the earth's four-legged creatures and reptiles and birds of the sky. A voice said to him: "Get up, Peter! Slaughter, then eat!" He answered, "Sir, it is unthinkable! I have never eaten anything unclean impure in my life." The voice was heard a second time:

"What God has purified, you are not to call unclean." This happened three times; then the object was snatched up into the sky. (Acts 10:11-16)

As Peter emerged from his ecstasy, the messengers from Cornelius arrived, detailing the vision of their commander. Instantly Peter returned with them to Caesarea. He told Cornelius and the friends who had assembled in his home that now he was certain that the kingdom of heaven was open to all men. He was certain that God had no favorites, and that His chosen people were those who feared Him and practiced righteousness. As we have seen, Peter was still talking when "the Holy Spirit descended upon all who were listening." The converts were baptized on the spot.

Peter was criticized by the Judeo-Christians, but silenced most of his opposition when he recounted his vision. Friction between Jewish and gentile converts to Christianity was to continue for decades. James the Righteous, who headed the Christian community of Jerusalem, insisted that *all* gentile converts undergo circumcision and keep all the Jewish traditions. Paul insisted that this was not necessary, since no one could satisfactorily keep the law anyway, and one was saved through the grace of Christ and not by works.

Around A.D. 49 there took place what is known as the Council of Jerusalem. Peter convened the presbyters, or priests, of the Christian community in Jerusalem and their leader, or bishop, James, as well as the other apostles. Whether all the Twelve were present at this time is not certain. The only one of their name who is mentioned is John. Peter came out in favor of Paul. Turning to James and the Jerusalem hierarchy, he said, "Why, then, do you put God to the test by trying to place on the shoulders of these converts a yoke which neither we nor our fathers were able to bear? Our belief is rather that we are saved by the favor of the Lord Jesus and so are they." (Acts 15:10-11) The Jerusalem Council decided that all gentile converts were to be bound to the Old Testament commandments concerning sexual purity, but that the only dietary and ritual restrictions to be imposed were abstention from drinking blood and eating anything that had been strangled or offered to idols.

This was not the end of the controversy. Peter complicated matters himself a few years later when he was visiting the Christians at Antioch. He had been taking his meals with the gentile Christians there until some priests came from Jerusalem and insisted that Peter abide by the Jewish regulation that forbade Jews to eat with gentiles. Apparently, James the Righteous and his followers assumed that whatever Jewish regulations had not been specifically discussed at the Council of Jerusalem should be retained. This was certainly not in the spirit of the council, but throughout history people have manifested the ability to interpret agreements so that they reflect their own point of view. Peter, no doubt for the sake of peace, began to take his meals apart from the gentiles when the Jacobean party arrived. We do not know all the facts, but it was a rather unfortunate decision on the part of Peter, as he was apparently undermining his own work at Jerusalem. Perhaps he was making an attempt to compromise. Paul scolded Peter for giving in to James. "If you who are a Jew are living according to Gentile ways rather than Jewish, by what logic do you force the Gentiles to adopt Jewish ways?" (Gal. 2:14) Apparently, Peter had himself ceased from keeping all the Jewish laws. Since the matter of eating with gentiles had not been taken up by the Jerusalem Council, Peter was embarrassed when he was criticized by the Jewish Christians. Paul made it clear, however, that these regulations had originated not from

Moses, but from rabbis who had legislated all sorts of regulations governing even the most trivial aspects of Jewish life. He explained that they were not essential to salvation and should never be insisted upon, even at the price of keeping peace.

How Peter reacted is not known, but we can be certain that the incident did not make him a bitter enemy of Paul, as some commentators maintain. At the end of his life, Peter wrote of Paul as "our beloved brother," and commended his writings to all believers. (II Peter 3:15-16)

These events give a picture of Peter's leadership. It is clear that he was the head of the Christian Church. James the Righteous was the head, or bishop, of the Christian congregation in Jerusalem, and perhaps the head of the college of priests. Paul was now the head of the mission to the gentiles in Greece and Asia Minor, which included most of the Hellenistic wing of the Church. Peter was the overseer of the entire Church. It was he who apparently assigned the other apostles to their various charges. He did not rule as a monarch or dictator, however, but with the consensus of the entire apostolic college. If Peter wanted to insist, his ruling was accepted by his colleagues, although he normally operated by discussion and compromise. It was necessary to take into account the very strong personalities and positions of such colleagues as James the Righteous and Paul. Peter could be argued with and made to change his mind if he was convinced that he was wrong. In his first epistle, Peter described himself not as the overseer of the Church, but as a "fellow elder" with the presbyters (or priests) to whom he was writing, urging them to lead their flocks, not as tyrants or overlords, but by being good examples. (I Pt. 5:1-3)

By the time of the Council of Jerusalem, Peter was no longer headquartered in Jerusalem. In order to understand his movement, we have to go back to A.D. 41. Herod

Agrippa I, who was already King of Galilee and several other Palestinian principalities, was created King of Judea, Samaria and Idumaea by the Emperor Claudius. Thus, the jurisdiction that had once been governed by Pontius Pilate passed to Agrippa's control. Agrippa, who had been an intimate of the cruel and depraved Emperor Caligula (recently assassinated), was evidently violently hostile to Christianity. With the support of the Sadducees on the Sanhedrin, in A.D. 42 or 43, he began a vicious campaign against the Christians in his kingdom. James, the brother of John, was beheaded. Shortly afterward, Peter was arrested and thrown into prison to await trial and almost certain death. One night, however, chained between two soldiers, with two more standing guard outside the cell, Peter found the room ablaze with light. In the midst of the light a celestial being ordered him to get up. The chains fell from his wrists on their own accord. Peter thought that he was dreaming until he found himself alone on a deserted Jerusalem street in the middle of the night. Hurrying to a house where a service of worship was in progress, he stayed long enough to establish the fact that he was safe, then left town. Luke says only that he went "elsewhere." Perhaps, in order to ensure his safety and to keep his friends from having to lie to protect him, Peter did not tell anyone where he was going.

Agrippa, who in a rage ordered the death of Peter's guards, died shortly afterward from an attack of dysentery, evidently visited upon him by God because of his blasphemous arrogance. Peter seemed never to have returned to Jerusalem to stay. Eusebius states that Peter, at this time, divided the accessible parts of the world among the apostles for personal evangelism. As superintendent of the apostolic college, Peter spent many years traveling throughout the Near East. He visited the Christian communities which were springing up all over that area, preaching, teaching, and making sure that the new converts fell into no heresy.

Peter preached extensively in Asia Minor. His first epistle is addressed to the Christians of Pontus, Galatia, Cappadocia, Asia and Bithynia — all regions of that area which is now the nation of Turkey. Peter also preached at Corinth some time prior to A.D. 54. Located in Greece, the Corinth of that time had been founded by Julius Caesar about a hundred years earlier. Corinth was an important business and commercial center. Its population was multinational, multiracial, and noted for its immorality. When Paul wrote his first epistle to the Corinthians around A.D. 54, the Church there had become fragmented into parties who put their loyalty to their favorite leaders above their loyalty to Jesus Christ. It was situations like this that Peter, Paul and the other apostles sought to alleviate.

Peter also resided for a time in Antioch. A large city of about a million people, it was located in what is now the nation of Syria, about seventeen miles east of the Mediterranean coast. Many of its streets were paved with marble and lined with colonnades, and there were many theaters, temples, baths and marketplaces. Antioch even had a system of night-lighting that historian Alan Bouquet described as "almost as effective" as the streetlights of the twentieth century.[2] It was the capital of the province of the East and a center of Greek culture. The people were mostly Syrian, with large Greek and Jewish minorities. St. Gregory the Great, who reigned as pope between A.D. 590 and 604, wrote that Peter stayed at Antioch for seven years and established an episcopal see there. If this is so, although there had been a thriving Christian community there, Peter organized it along lines of Church policy and ordained a bishop. The second-century *Constitutions of the Holy Apostles* identified the bishop as Eodius.

Peter apparently traveled elsewhere, too. George F.

Jowett, in his book *The Drama of the Lost Apostles,* cites obscure apocryphal records to contend that Peter preached in Gaul and in Britain. At least one scholar contends that Peter's second epistle, written just before his death, was in fact composed in Britain. It is possible that Peter traveled there, as Britain was by now a part of the Roman Empire, but there is no firm documentation.

During all his travels, Peter was apparently accompanied by his wife, Perpetua. Nineteenth-century French Catholic scholar Abbé Constant Fouard suggested that Peter's wife played an active role in evangelical work, preaching and even baptizing converts and leading prayer meetings. This, however, was mere speculation. The character of Peter's wife was likely recalled in Peter's advice to Christian women in his first epistle. He advised married women to "obey your husbands," to shun jewelry and lavish clothing, and instead seek "the hidden character of the heart, expressed in the unfading beauty of a calm and gentle disposition. This is precious in God's eyes." He urged them to imitate "the holy women of past ages," who were "reliant on God and obedient to their husbands." As an example, he cited Sarah, "who was subject to Abraham and called him her master." (I Pt. 3:1-6)

Peter eventually went to Rome and lived there during his latter years. Nobody knows exactly when he arrived there, and it is possible that he visited the Eternal City several times before he settled there. Paul does not mention Peter in his Letter to the Romans, which he wrote about A.D. 57, which leads most scholars to believe that Peter was not in Rome at this time. It is possible that Peter had established his home in Rome, but happened to be out of town when Paul wrote.

In Rome, Peter probably made his home in the sizable Jewish community there. In those days, the apostles always went first to the Jewish community to preach the

Gospel in the synagogues. Then they would branch out to the gentiles. There were between 30,000 and 40,000 Jews living in Rome in the first century. When Peter and Perpetua arrived, they found many of the inhabitants, both Jew and gentile, very much taken with the teachings of a cultist known as Simon Magus (Simon the Magician). A native of the town of Gittho in Samaria, years before he had seen the powerful effects of the Holy Spirit poured out on the converts there, and offered Peter money for this gift. Several years later he went to Rome where he appealed to the bored and effete with an occult and immoral religion. Eusebius points out that Simon was "the prime author of every heresy." Through demonic collaboration, he was able to counterfeit some of the miracles worked by Christ and the apostles. Without going into any details, Eusebius calls Simon's doctrines "unholy" and "sordid." The Magus traveled about with a female companion named Helen. Simon Magus and Helen encouraged their followers to worship them with incense, sacrifices and libations. Involved in their cult were "more secret rites," which, according to Eusebius, had to do with "degradations" so "appalling," that he deemed their description unfit to put into writing.[3]

Eusebius tells us that it was expressly to combat Simon Magus that Simon Peter came to live in Rome. "Clad in divine armor, like a noble captain of God, he brought the precious merchandise of the spiritual light from the East to those in the West, preaching the good news of light itself and the soul-saving word, the proclamation of the Kingdom of Heaven. Thus, when the divine word had made its home [among the people of Rome], Simon's power was extinguished and destroyed at once with the man himself."[4]

Eusebius did not make it clear exactly what happened to Simon Magus. According to *The Acts of Peter,* an ancient historical novel dating from the second century, the Magus, through the power of Satan, was able to levitate, rising off his feet high into the air. He challenged Peter publicly, declaring before a large crowd that he was about to levitate above the Roman skyline. Then he dared Jesus, if He were Lord, to stop him. Simon proceeded to levitate many feet above the ground, while the huge throngs looked on with amazement. Peter prayed out loud that Jesus might vindicate His faith, and promptly Simon Magus plummeted to the ground and broke his leg. Before he could limp away, the crowd, now convinced that Jesus was Lord and Simon was only a phony, stoned the false prophet to death.[5]

Peter's popularity increased rapidly with many converts made in Rome. Even many pagans were attracted to this man who left a reputation for being "humble, meek, gentle, tender, loving, and lovely."[6] Eventually, perhaps in the early A.D. 60s, the Roman converts begged Peter's secretary, John Mark, to put into writing "a summary of the instruction they had received by word of mouth." Mark, apparently a Jew, native to Jerusalem, was a sort of son to Peter and his wife. Mark had originally traveled with Paul and Barnabas and been the unwitting cause of a rift between the two apostles. Barnabas had wanted to take Mark with them on another journey, but Paul refused to take him because he felt that Mark had deserted them earlier. Mark had for some years worked with Peter, and would shortly be sent to Alexandria, Egypt, to establish an episcopal see there and die a martyr. Without consulting Peter, Mark wrote what became the earliest of the Gospels. Eusebius declares that Peter found out what Mark had done only by "revelation of the spirit." When he learned of the enthusiasm with which it was received by Roman Christians, Peter was delighted. He then authorized its reading in all Christian churches worldwide.[7]

Storm clouds were gathering, however. Since A.D. 54, the Roman emperor had been Nero. For the first few years after his accession to power at the age of sixteen, Nero, under the influence of his tutor, the philosopher Lucius Annaeus Seneca, governed justly. As he grew older the young emperor broke away from the influence of Seneca (whom he later put to death) and began to earn a reputation for "wantonness, lust, extravagance, avarice, and cruelty."[8] Nero was about five feet, four inches tall with light blond hair, freckles, a potbelly, and "bird legs." He reportedly indulged in every kind of sexual perversion, and even committed incest with his mother, the immoral Agrippina. He also castrated young boys for purposes of sexual perversion. Suspicious and brutal, according to Suetonius, he "showed neither discrimination nor moderation in putting to death whomever he pleased on any pretext whatsoever."[9] Most ominous for the Christian community, Nero "utterly despised" all religions except that of the Syrian Venus. He later showed his contempt for that cult by publicly urinating on the image of the goddess.

On the night of July 19, A.D. 64, fire broke out in a wooden shed at the foot of the Caelian and Palatine hills in Rome, and spread to the small shops nearby. Within hours, much of the city was engulfed by flames which burned out of control for nine days, destroying two thirds of Rome and killing hundreds. Nero, who was in the city of Anzio at the time and had no part in its destruction, blamed the Christians for the disaster. Had not Peter and Paul publicly proclaimed that the world would end in fire? Therefore, they must have been responsible. He denounced Christianity as a "deadly superstition," and accused Christians of being haters of the human race and perpetrators of such crimes as drinking the blood of babies in Holy Communion. Thus he marked the Church for extermination.

The Christian holocaust seems not to have come immediately after the fire. Doubtless Nero and his government were too busy for the first year or so rebuilding the city to do much more than denounce the "pernicious superstition." Peter knew that the persecution was coming when he penned what is known as his first catholic, or universal, epistle — that is, a formal letter for general circulation. This was sent to the Christian communities in Asia Minor.

Peter told his brethren that they must expect to suffer, and that for many of them "the end of all things is at hand." (I Pt. 4:7, RSV) Nevertheless, they were to "remain calm so that you will be able to pray." (I Pt. 4:7) No matter what happened, Christians were to live virtuously and lovingly, holding to their faith and waiting for the "imperishable inheritance, incapable of fading or defilement, which is kept in heaven for you" (I Pt. 1:4), joyful even though "you may for a time have to suffer the distress of many trials." (I Pt. 1:6) In earthly adversity, in the face of death, Peter declared that the child of God should look to his reward in heaven and be patient until "the God of all grace, who called you to his everlasting glory in Christ, will himself restore, confirm, strengthen, and establish those who have suffered a little while." (I Pt. 5:10)

Peter wrote a second epistle later. Almost all modern scholars consider it inauthentic, written a century after Peter died. Eusebius wrote that only Peter's first epistle was genuine and that the other one "we have been taught to regard as uncanonical; many, however, have thought it valuable and have honored it with a place among the other Scriptures."[10] Why he felt this epistle was "disputed" he did not say, except that he had been "taught." The Church, however, when it defined the canon, declared the second epistle authentic, and one must assume that this was on the basis of some information which was extant then, but is not available today. Otherwise, if the epistle were not the work of Peter, it would be a forgery, and have no place in Scripture, no matter how many words of wisdom it contains. Modern scholars have explained that it was not uncommon in ancient times for unknown writers to attribute their own works to well-known authors of the past, to ensure that they would attract attention. This was forgery, pure and simple. Murder, abortion, infanticide, fornication and homosexuality were as common among Romans as forgery, but no one in his right mind would imagine that the apostles and their successors condoned those acts. The author of II Peter clearly stated that he was Simon Peter, an apostle of Jesus Christ. He described the Transfiguration as an eyewitness, and spoke of Paul as his friend and contemporary. If this epistle were not the work of Peter, it would be a bald-faced lie and not a sacred writing.

Peter, who knew that he was about to die, wrote to all Christians everywhere, reminding them to hold fast to the things that he had taught them, reminding them that he had not devised "cleverly concocted myths," but had spoken out of his own experience. He reminded them that the teachings of the apostles originated not from their own insights but from the impulse of the Holy Spirit. (II Pt. 1:20)

He also addressed the delay in Christ's return. Many, if not most, early Christians expected Christ to return in their lifetime. Even St. Paul did, at least for a time. By the end of Peter's life, more than three decades had passed since the Lord's Ascension, and many were asking, "Where is that promised coming of his? Our forefathers have been laid to rest, but everything stays just as it was when the world was created." (II Pt. 3:4) Peter answered by saying that Christ would come in His own time, and "in the Lord's eyes, one day is as a thousand years and a thousand years are as a day. The Lord does not delay in keeping his promise — though some consider it 'delay.' Rather, he shows you generous patience, since he wants none to perish but all to come to repentance." (II Pt. 3:8-9) Thus, with a message about God's love and faithfulness, Peter urged the faithful to grow in grace and in the knowledge of the Lord and Savior Jesus Christ, and to give glory to Him "now and to the day of eternity." (II Pt. 3:18)

It must have been in A.D. 65 or 66 that the Neronian persecution began in earnest. The Roman historian P. Cornelius Tacitus tells us:

First Nero had self-acknowledged Christians arrested. Then, on their information, large numbers of others were condemned. . . .Their deaths were made farcical. Dressed in wild animals' skins, they were torn to pieces by dogs, or crucified, or made into torches to be ignited after dark as substitutes for daylight.[11]

Paul was beheaded in A.D. 66. The massacre continued at least until Nero's deposition and suicide in June, A.D. 68. As to the number of martyrs, both Roman and Christian historians have simply said "large numbers." The victims could have numbered in the hundreds, thousands, or (less likely) tens of thousands. A substantial portion of the Church was martyred during these years, but converts were made as many pagans were impressed by the courage and cheerfulness with which the martyrs met their gruesome ends.

The *Acts of Peter* contends that the Christians in Rome feared that the Church would become extinct if anything happened to Peter, and urged the apostles to flee Rome and go into hiding. Persuaded to do this, Peter, in disguise, on the outside of the city, had a vision of Christ.

The Lord was walking toward Rome carrying a cross. "Why are you coming here?" asked Peter. The Lord replied that He was going to Rome to be crucified again since he, Peter, seemed intent on running away from his duty. Shamed at his cowardice, Peter immediately turned back to Rome.

Eventually both Peter and his wife were arrested. Tradition holds that Peter was kept nine months in a noisome and fetid dungeon called the Tullian Keep, chained to a column. The Roman authorities had to change guards continually, because Peter was converting them almost as soon as they were assigned to him. Finally, on a date often given as June 29 in a year Eusebius maintained was A.D. 67, Peter was crucified.

Clement of Alexandria recorded that as he saw Perpetua led away to her death, Peter "was glad that her call had come and that she was returning home, . . . [and] in the most encouraging and comforting of tones he called her by name and said, 'My dear, remember the Lord.' "[12] Peter was crucified upside down, apparently at his own request. Most ancient authorities said that he gave no reason for this request. Perhaps he expected that, upside down, he would lose consciousness more quickly.

So ended the earthly career of the rock upon whom Christ built His Church, a very human man, at times childish, impulsive, even cowardly. But a man who, when he walked in the strength of the Lord, was a mighty champion of the faith.

Peter was not normally a cowardly or wayward man, but during the course of his long and busy life he met many challenges that were too great for any man to face alone. When he relied on his own strength, Peter made a fool of himself. When he relied on the Lord, he was always victorious.

3

Andrew: Second fiddle

THROUGHOUT history, being the son, daughter, brother, sister, niece or nephew of a very famous person has often hindered the individual concerned from achieving any significant recognition on his own. This was almost certainly the case with Andrew, "the brother of Simon Peter." That worthy man was mentioned twelve times in the Bible, but almost always he was identified as "Simon Peter's brother," as if the reader could not be expected to know who he was except through his relationship to the "Prince of Apostles."

The fact that Andrew lived his life in the shadow of his brother has led the fertile imaginations of many commentators and writers, starved for facts, to conclude that he was perhaps less intelligent, less able or even less holy than Peter. There is really no basis for such a conclusion, but what does the Bible tell us about St. Andrew?

Andrew figured in but seven incidents in the New Testament. John, in the first chapter of his Gospel, writes that Andrew was originally a disciple of John the Baptist, and was urged to seek Jesus himself. This Andrew did, and, convinced that he found the Messiah, hurried to tell his brother Peter. Both Matthew and Mark record how Jesus called Andrew, along with Peter, James and John, while they were fishing in the Sea of Galilee. Luke tells how Andrew was one of the first of the disciples to be chosen as one of the apostles by the Lord. John recounts Andrew's role in bringing the boy with the loaves and fishes to Jesus, who multiplied them to feed a crowd of more than five thousand. John also recounts how Andrew, along with his friend Philip, approached Jesus in behalf of some Greek inquirers. Mark identifies Andrew as one of those who questioned Jesus about the end of the world, and Luke indicates that he was with the other apostles and the family of Jesus in the "upper room" immediately following Jesus' Ascension.

Nothing more is said about Andrew in Scripture. From the meager information we have, we are able to learn some tentative facts about Andrew's character and personality. We must be tentative when we remember that the information recounted about Andrew is only coincidental. The evangelists spoke about him not for the purpose of revealing any details about his personality, but to illustrate some word or action of Jesus. There is always the possibility that the incidents in which Andrew figure are not at all characteristic of him. For lack of further evidence, however, we must draw our conclusions from the facts at hand.

First, we learn something about Andrew through the fact that he was a brother of Peter. Presumably he was a full brother and thus born in Bethsaida, a child of Jonah and Joanna. The name "Andrew" is Greek and means "manly." Perhaps his parents were sufficiently Hellenized to give a Greek name to one or more of their children; perhaps Andrew had a Hebrew name, which had been forgotten and was, like Simon, given a surname by Jesus, in this case because of a courageous disposition. It was unlikely, however, that Jesus would have given a Greek name to one of His followers (remember that Peter was called "Kefos" in Hebrew). If Andrew had taken a Greek name himself later in life, it was likely that one of the evangelists would have mentioned his original name. So, it seems likely that Andrew was so named by his parents, who did not consider it sacrilegious to give a Jewish boy a Greek name.

Presumably Andrew had an education similar to Peter's and, like him, went into the fishing business at an early age. Unlike Peter, Andrew apparently never married, since he lived with Peter and his family at the beginning of his ministry. This was highly unusual for the time, but it seems clear that by the first century some devout Jews, like John the Baptist, were adopting a celibate lifestyle.

We learn something about Andrew from the first chapter of St. John, who wrote that Andrew was first a disciple of John the Baptist. At the time the Baptist pointed out Jesus to Andrew, the two sons of Jonah were some eighty miles away from their home in Capernaum. They were obviously committed enough to the prophet to take at least some time off from their work to follow him.

What being a disciple of the Baptist entailed is not particularly clear. Although Andrew and Peter gave up some of their time to travel with him, John evidently did not insist that they give up everything to follow him. Some scholars have noted some similarity between the teachings of John and those of the Essenes. An important denomination of Judaism, this group had a community at Qumran, near the Dead Sea. It was also near the spot where John did much of his baptizing. They led rigorous, self-denying lives, encouraging personal holiness, purity, and celibacy, urging their hearers to fly from the coming retribution. Some scholars felt that John and his disciples were part of this group; others felt that John may have been influenced by the Essenes, but was not at this time a part of any of their communities.

John (the apostle) recorded that one day the Baptist was standing with Andrew and another disciple when Jesus appeared, requesting baptism from John. "Look!

There is the Lamb of God!'' John said, encouraging his followers to talk with the man whom he tentatively identified as Israel's long-awaited Messiah. (Jn. 1:36) We are struck at the humility of the Baptist, who was not jealous of Jesus or begrudged the fact that the Lord's ministry was to supplant his own.

Jesus welcomed Andrew and his friend and invited them into the house where He was lodging, and the three spent most of the day together. When Andrew left Jesus later that day, he had no doubt that he had been with the Messiah, and his first impulse was to find Peter and tell him about his experience. When Andrew introduced Simon Peter to Jesus, the Lord immediately indicated that it was Peter who would be chief among His apostles, not Andrew. Like the Baptist, Andrew must have been a man of great humility. It was he who had first discovered Jesus, and Peter had come to meet Him only at his brother's urging. Yet the Messiah seemed to consider Peter more important than Andrew.

Why this was the case we can only guess. It was quite likely that Peter was the more outgoing and aggressive of the two. Age also doubtless played a role, too. It was commonly accepted in that society that the oldest brother was given precedence over the younger ones. There is no evidence that Andrew ever resented Peter's preeminence.

We next glimpse Andrew after the Baptist's arrest, when he and his brother, along with James and John, encountered Jesus by the Sea of Galilee and were granted the miraculous draught of fish. As we have seen, it was at this time that Jesus insisted that the four men devote all their time to being His disciples. From that point on, Andrew gave up all involvement in his business to spend his time in the company of Jesus. The apostolic college was formally established later, when, after a night of prayer, Jesus assembled all His disciples and chose the Twelve to take His teachings to the world. Andrew was among the first called. Many think that he was the very first.

Andrew figured prominently in the feeding of "The Five Thousand." At that time, Jesus was being pursued by vast crowds of people. After crossing the Sea of Galilee and landing at the town of Tiberias on the western shore, he went with his disciples to the top of a mountain to pray. Soon it was apparent that a vast multitude was converging on Him. Jesus, pitying them because "they were like sheep without a shepherd" (Mk. 6:34), began to teach them. The evangelists recorded that there were five thousand men there, not counting women and children. (Mt. 14:21) Thus there must have been well over 15,000 in the crowd, probably many more. Jesus preached at great length, till it was evening. Realizing that the people came from all over Palestine, some of the disciples were concerned about the lateness of the hour. It was probably too late for many of them to walk home, and before long it would be too late for them to find food in the nearby villages. When pressed to dismiss the crowds, Jesus replied by telling His disciples to feed the people. Philip was horrified, pointing out that in order for everyone to get even a scrap, they would have to spend an astronomical sum of money, which they did not have.

Andrew, however, did not protest or object. He simply went into the crowd, trying to find out what was available in the way of food. He reappeared with a small boy who had only five barley loaves and a couple of fish. Apparently, nobody else had brought anything to eat. "This is all I could find, Master," Andrew said. "What are five loaves and two fishes among so many thousands?" Jesus, however, bade the people sit, blessed the loaves and fish and multiplied them so that everyone had so much as he could eat, and even then had twelve baskets of bread left over. (Jn. 6:13)

This tells us something about Andrew. He had a deep trust in his Lord and an awareness that Jesus was Master, even over the laws of nature. Philip dismissed the possibility of feeding the crowd, but Andrew realized that as long as the Lord was near, there was a solution. "Lord, You want us to feed these people. I've done my best to see if any of the people brought lunches with them and all I could find was this meager offering. Just as You provided us with fish when there were none in the waters before, I am confident that You can supply this crowd. How, I don't know. But I know that Your grace is sufficient for every need." This was Andrew's attitude. He knew that to serve his Master he had to go all out to do his best and leave the deficit of his human capabilities to the Lord.

The apostle John also recounted another incident that brought light to bear on his colleague's personality. Shortly before the Lord's arrest and crucifixion, Philip was approached by several Greeks who wished to speak to Jesus. This was something of a "sticky wicket," because it was not then clear that Jesus' messiahship extended beyond Israel. Philip did not know what to do, so he came to Andrew about the problem. What should they do? Should they send the Greeks away, saying, "We're sorry, but our Master does not deal with gentiles," or should the apostles lead the people to Jesus and risk embarrassing both them as well as the Master if He should refuse to see them? Apparently Andrew decided that they should go ahead and take the men to Jesus. The Lord was willing to see them, since His words expressed the offer of salvation to all the world: "If anyone would serve me let him follow me; where I am, there will my servant be. If anyone serves me, him the Father will honor." (Jn. 12:26)

These few incidents tend to show that Andrew was a kindly, mild, unassuming man, friendly, approachable and very trusting. He was not apparently aggressive or ambitious, not the sort of fellow who was unhappy and fulfilled unless he was in charge. He was extremely eager to tell others about Jesus. Did he resent playing "second fiddle" to his brother Peter and his friend John? Perhaps he overcame such feelings, if they ever existed, through submission to the will of God. Perhaps he never had such feelings, but was concerned solely in being and doing what Jesus wanted, whether that brought prominence or obscurity. There are some people who, through their devotion to Christ, attain such equanimity of spirit that ambition means nothing to them and their only desire is doing God's will, and their only fear is losing Him. This was Andrew's attitude.

What became of St. Andrew after Pentecost? Scripture is silent except to say that the apostles (or most of them) remained in Jerusalem at least until the persecution by Herod Agrippa. Thus we might surmise that Andrew made Jerusalem his home base at least until A.D. 42. Doubtless he continued to live with Peter and his family, and probably accompanied his older brother on his various journeys around Palestine. At this time the Church continued to grow in Transjordan (modern Jordan), Arabia (the far northwestern portion of what is now called Saudi Arabia), Phoenicia (modern Lebanon), and Osroene (southeastern Turkey), and other Aramaic-speaking areas with heavy Jewish populations.

Eusebius stated that Andrew's primary field of activity was among the Scythians. Other sources indicated Pontus, Bithynia and, finally, Greece. On the basis of the meager information we have, we can draw a general and tentative picture of Andrew's activities from A.D. 42 until his death twenty-seven years later.

Andrew perhaps remained in Jerusalem after Peter escaped from prison in A.D. 42 or 43. It is likely that he rejoined him later in Pontus, a region of what is now northern Turkey that borders on the southeastern end of the Black Sea.

The Acts of the Apostles sketches the manner in which Andrew likely took leave of the brethren at Jerusalem. Although Luke wrote mainly of Paul, we can assume that the other apostles operated similarly. We can assume that before Andrew set out on his long journey, the apostles and other Church leaders still in Jerusalem met with him. For a full day they would fast and pray before bidding him Godspeed. It is highly unlikely that Andrew traveled alone, since the followers of Jesus usually traveled in pairs, if not in larger groups. If Andrew did not leave Jerusalem with Peter, it is likely that he left with one or more younger disciples. Perhaps Peter, after his arrest, had slipped out of Jerusalem alone, and then sent for Andrew along with other members of his immediate family.

After an arduous journey, partially by boat, but mainly by foot, Andrew and his party finally reached Peter either in Sinope or Amisus (the two main towns on the Black Sea). These towns would not have been totally strange to Peter and Andrew. There were many Jews there and many of the people made their living by fishing. We can be sure that the brothers lived in the Jewish community and attended one of the local synagogues, where they proclaimed the Gospel of Christ to worshipers. If their converts were not able to support them materially, it is likely that the brothers worked, at least part of the time, in the fishing industry, just as Paul worked as a manufacturer of tents.

Andrew and Peter perhaps remained partners for over a decade. They moved westward into the area known as Bithynia, also on the Black Sea. It is clear that the brothers at times separated. There is no mention of Andrew at Antioch or at the Council of Jerusalem, but this does not mean that he was not there. Andrew, according to the third-century *Teaching of the Twelve Apostles*, consecrated bishops in Nicomedia in Nicaea, known as the "golden city of Bithynia." He allegedly established an episcopal see in Byzantium (later called Constantinople, then Istanbul), which later became the most important center of the Eastern Orthodox Church.

At some point Andrew ministered to the Scythians. These blond, blue-eyed people lived on the northern and eastern shores of the Black Sea, outside the boundaries of the Roman Empire. They were evidently quite primitive people. The Jewish historian Josephus considered them "little different from wild beasts."[1] They evidently practiced cannibalism. In this mission exclusively to gentiles, Andrew, according to one tradition, was accompanied not by Peter, but by Matthias. Why they decided to go to this region is not known, but it is possible that there were some Jews who ran a trading post in that region. Perhaps Andrew knew Scythians in Pontus and Bithynia who were converted, who urged him to take the good news to their family and friends in their homeland. How successful Andrew was in evangelizing in the "developing nation" of Scythia we do not know. There are traditions that he rescued Matthias from being eaten by cannibals, and succeeded in converting a number of these people.

Probably in the early A.D. 50s Andrew moved south and west again. There are traditions that he preached for a while in Armenia, a kingdom on the southeastern corner of the Black Sea, just south of Scythia, before moving westward again across Asia Minor. There he would have visited the churches that he and Peter had founded in Pontus and Bithynia, perhaps joining with his brother once more before crossing over into Greece and preaching in the cities of Perinthus, Philippi and Thessalonica. Peter perhaps accompanied him as far as Patrae, then decided that he should go to Rome while Andrew remained there.

When we speak of Andrew's ministry in Patrae, we are on firm ground. Nearly all traditions agree that the apostle worked there for many years and was martyred there. We can guess that Andrew arrived there in the A.D. 50s . He was then in his late forties and evidently decided to settle there for life. He probably made a home in the Jewish community with a disciple or two, but would make frequent trips to other parts of Greece. Tradition records trips to Corinth, Philippi, Sparta and Megara.

A third-century historical novel called the *Acts of Andrew*, which Eusebius denounced because it contained heretical doctrine, possibly preserves (in exaggerated form) some incidents of Andrew's ministry there. For instance, there is the story of the exorcism Andrew performed upon a young Roman soldier named Varianus. When the apostle approached, an alien voice issued from the soldier's throat, bellowing, "O Varianus, what have I done to you that you should send me this God-fearing man?" At once Varianus was hurled to the ground by an unseen force and began to foam at the mouth in an epileptoid seizure. As his fellow-soldiers held him up, Andrew quietly healed him. Restored to himself, Varianus took off his uniform and cast it at Andrew's feet, despite warnings from his comrades about the severe punishment meted out to deserters. Varianus was not swayed, saying that he preferred "the garment of the immortal king of ages."[2]

According to one of the legendary accounts, Andrew was in Philippi when the Neronian persecution broke out there. Like Daniel, Andrew was thrown to the lions and escaped when the beasts would not attack him. It is certainly plausible to believe that in the last years of his life Andrew was harassed by the Roman authorities as well as hostile pagan and Jewish hearers. On at least one occasion he barely escaped with his life.

Andrew's death apparently resulted not so much from

the official policy of the Roman government, but from the anger of a local governor. Patrae was located on the northern shore of the large peninsula known as the Peleponnesus, which was connected to the Greek mainland only by the tiny isthmus of Corinthia. A medium-sized city overlooking a body of water called the Gulf of Patrae, the city had a governor appointed by Rome.

It seemed the wife of the governor was deathly ill. Pronounced incurable by her doctors, and aware of Andrew's reputation as a healer, she sent for him and was healed immediately, and became a Christian. So did her husband's brother Stratocles. Aegeates, the governor, wanted no part of the new religion, and considered the conversion of his wife an alienation of affection. Sometime in the fall of A.D. 69, he arrested Andrew and imprisoned him. As had happened with Peter two years earlier, Andrew's jailers had to be changed constantly, since they were converted almost as soon as they were assigned to the holy man. Finally, on November 28, A.D. 69, Aegeates gave orders that Andrew be crucified.

Despite the protests of his wife and brother, Aegeates had Andrew hauled to the seashore and tied to a cross. He gave instructions that the condemned man not be nailed, so that Andrew could die a slow, lingering death of exposure and exhaustion. The governor even expressed the hope that Andrew would be gradually torn apart by the wild dogs that foraged about the seashore. The dogs, however, never had a chance, because the news of Andrew's crucifixion attracted a huge crowd which surrounded the cross day and night. Despite his torments, the aging apostle — he was then at least in his early sixties — managed to summon the strength to talk about the things of God. The *Acts of Andrew* contended that more than 2,000 people were converted by Andrew while he hung on the cross on the shores of the Gulf of Patrae.

Meanwhile, there was turmoil at the gubernatorial mansion. A huge crowd gathered around the house and demanded that Aegeates free this man who was innocent of any capital offense. Finally, the governor agreed at least to speak to Andrew, whom he had never met before.

The governor confronted the holy man on his cross by the seashore. Andrew, however, would not hear of release. It was not stated in the *Acts of Andrew*, but perhaps Aegeates in real life agreed to release him only on condition that he leave town or stop preaching about Christ. "Let no one release me," Andrew said. "For there has been allotted me this destiny — to depart out of the body and live with the Lord, with whom I am even being crucified."[3] Aegeates agreed to spare Andrew unconditionally, but, while being cut down, the old, exhausted man murmured, "Jesus Christ, whom I have seen, whom I have, whom I love, in whom I am and will be, receive me in peace into thy eternal tabernacles, that through my exodus the many who are akin in nature to me may enter to Thee and rest in Thy majesty."[4] He died on November 30, A.D. 69.

St. Andrew is associated not only with Greece, but also with Russia and Scotland. Because he ministered in Scythia, which is now part of the U.S.S.R., St. Andrew was named patron saint of Russia by the Russian Orthodox Church. In A.D. 750, Hungus, King of Picts (in what is now Scotland), was about to do battle with the English when, the night before the battle, he dreamt that St. Andrew promised him victory. The next day, above Hungus' camp, there was seen in the sky a shining cross, shaped like an X. The Picts advanced into battle shouting, "St. Andrew, our patron, be our guide!" and won. Ever since that time St. Andrew has been the patron saint of the Scots, and his symbol has been a cross shaped like an X.

Although Andrew may not have been as outgoing and dynamic as his brother Peter, he was a courageous man who spent his life traveling to bring the good news of Christ to those who sat in darkness. We hear little of his being a great preacher and orator, and it may be that he best operated on a one-to-one basis, telling about his Lord in conversation. Even so, he founded at least three episcopal sees and led, reportedly, thousands of people, Jew and gentile alike, to Christ.

4

The three Jameses and Jerusalem Christianity

THE name "St. James" is familiar to most Christians, but if asked to recount something about "him" most people would be at a loss. Many would unwittingly make one man of three, not realizing that there were three leaders of the early Church named James — all of them associated with Jerusalem. St. James the Great, the son of Zebedee and brother of John, was mentioned frequently in the Gospels, but, except in a passage in Acts recounting his death, nowhere else in the New Testament. St. James the Less, also an apostle, was the son of Alphaeus and his wife Mary. He was also a brother of St. Matthew, but nothing more was said of him in Scripture. We know the most about James the Righteous, who was the apparent author of the epistle bearing his name, and who was mentioned both in Acts and by Paul, but was not one of the Twelve. Nevertheless, he was a figure of towering importance, who seemed to exercise an authority equal, or almost equal, to Peter's. He was converted after the Resurrection and became the head of the Church in Jerusalem.

St. James the Great, the brother of John, was probably the most famous of these three men, but his renown stemmed more from association with his brother, and from his posthumous reputation as patron of Spain, than from any scriptural record. What the Bible says about him is meager indeed.

St. James the Great (Jacob bar Zebedee) was probably, like Peter, a native of Bethsaida in Galilee. If scholar William Steuart McBirnie was correct in his surmise that James was the father of the apostle Jude Thaddeus, he was in fact one of the oldest of the apostles, born not much later than 15 B.C., and in his forties at the time of his call. It is more likely, however, that James was not the father of Jude, and was perhaps just a year or two older than his brother John, and was born around the beginning of the Christian era. His father was identified in Scripture as the fisherman Zebedee, a partner of Peter in the fishing business. His mother was Salome, a sister of the Virgin Mary. How do we know this?

Each of the evangelists identified several women who stood beneath the cross during the Lord's Passion. Luke spoke merely of "the women who had accompanied him [Jesus] from Galilee." (Lk. 23:49) Mark, however, identified the women as (1) Mary Magdalene, (2) Mary, the mother of James the Less and Joses, and (3) Salome. (Mk. 15:40) Matthew named Mary Magdalene and Mary, the mother of James and Joses, and, without naming her, identified the third woman as the mother of Zebedee's sons. (Mt. 28:5) John stated that the mother of Jesus also stood beneath the cross, but, in addition, identified the same three ladies: (1) Mary Magdalene, (2) Mary, the wife of Cleopas, and (3) Jesus' mother's sister (her name was not given). (Jn. 19:25) It seems clear that (a) Salome, (b) the sister of the Virgin Mary, and (c) the mother of Zebedee's sons were the same woman. If this was so, James and John were first cousins to the Lord.

James and John, like their friends Peter and Andrew, were educated in Bethsaida until their early teens, then went to work with their father Zebedee. Zebedee owned at least one fishing vessel, and tradition has it that he was quite prosperous. A couple of apocryphal Gospels stated that Zebedee supplied fish to the high priestly family in Jerusalem. This would certainly explain why John was known to the high priest and able to obtain access for himself and Peter at the trial of Jesus.

There are some indications that Zebedee and Salome were, like their sons, disciples of John the Baptist. Certainly Salome readily embraced the teaching of Jesus and became one of a large circle of pious ladies who accompanied the Lord and the Twelve. Luke mentioned that there were "many" of these ladies who "were assisting them out of their means." (Lk. 8:3)

Although she was one of Jesus' benefactresses, an incident recorded by Matthew did not cast a very favorable light on Salome's comprehension of the purpose of her nephew's ministry. Once she approached Jesus and asked Him for a favor: when He became king, would He permit her two sons to have the privilege of sitting, "one at your right hand and the other at your left, in your kingdom"? (Mt. 20:21) Salome was thinking of Jesus' kingdom in the popular worldly sense. Like many Jews of the day, she expected the Messiah to be a political leader who would overthrow the Romans and make himself an earthly king. When this happened, she wanted Jesus to make His cousins second in power only to himself. Perhaps one might be prime minister and the other one minister of finance. Both of her sons were with her when she made the request. Jesus threw cold water on their expectations by telling them that they really did not know what they were asking for. "Can you drink the cup that I am about to drink?" He asked.

John and James, thinking that this cup was the cup of glory, cheerfully said that they could. "From the cup I drink of, you shall drink. But sitting at my right hand or my left is not mine to give. That is for those to whom it has been reserved by my Father." (Mt. 20:23) Little did

Salome and her sons know that the cup they sought to drink was the cup of suffering and humiliation.

St. James appeared in seven incidents in the New Testament. Matthew, Mark and Luke described how James, along with John, Peter and Andrew, were called by Jesus to leave their boats and follow Him. Many people assume that they had never seen Jesus before, but this was hardly the case. Jesus had met Peter and Andrew shortly before at one of John the Baptist's "evangelical crusades" at Bethabara. If James and John were not present then, the Lord had doubtless known them all their lives. Bethsaida was more than twenty-five miles from Nazareth, but it was likely that Mary and Salome and their families made periodic visits. What occurred by the Sea of Galilee was doubtless the formal call to the fishermen to devote themselves full-time to the Lord's service. Then, some time after that came the call to apostleship.

James was considered one of the "inner circle" of apostles, because on three occasions Jesus was described as taking him, John and Peter along with Him. These three men were present alone with Jesus when He raised from the dead the daughter of Jairus, the synagogue president; at the Transfiguration; and in the Garden of Gethsemane. Whether this intimacy occurred simply by happenstance, whether the three were closer because they were more developed spiritually, or whether they were closer because James and John were the Lord's close relatives and Peter was their close friend, it is impossible to say.

There were two incidents which cast light on James' character and temperament. Mark recounted that when Jesus selected the Twelve to be apostles and gave Simon the surname "Peter," he named James and John "Boanerges," which is Greek for "Sons of Thunder." Why?

An incident recorded by Luke which took place just

before the Passion may throw some light on this. En route to Jerusalem, Jesus and His sizable entourage stopped in a Samaritan village and tried in vain to find accommodations there. The relationship of Samaritan and Jew in the Holy Land in the first century was comparable to that between Arab and Jew in the twentieth century. When all the innkeepers (in a manner of speaking) displayed "No dogs and Jews" signs, James and John were furious and wanted Jesus to exact cosmic vengeance. "May we call down fire from heaven to burn them up?" they asked.

"You know not what manner of spirit you are of," said He. "For the Son of man is not come to destroy men's lives, but to save them!" (Lk. 9:54, KJV).

Many believed that James and John earned their surname from this incident. Perhaps on other occasions they urged Jesus to avenge himself on those who had mistreated Him by striking them dead with lightning bolts. James and John had seen their Master walk on water, and knew that even the wind and waves obeyed Him. They knew that He could use the elements in any way He chose. This is in keeping with the "seats of honor" incident. James and John originally saw Jesus' ministry as political, and originally saw violence against their opponents as an acceptable means to the desired end.

Philip Schaff had a more positive interpretation of *Boanerges*. He said that for a Jew of that time, "Son of Thunder" had the connotation "Voice of God." Thus he concluded that James and John were not *Boanerges* because of ferocity or fanaticism, but because of their "ardent temper, great strength, and vehemence of character."[1]

Probably both points of view are correct. James and John may originally have been men whose zeal bordered on fanaticism. It was through Jesus that they were rescued from degenerating into the type of religious terrorist who then, as now, is a curse to their part of the world. Later, with their fire and fervor directed into proper channels, the brothers grew into men who, uncompromising and outspoken, fearlessly proclaimed the truth bluntly and forthrightly.

The early Church referred to James as "James the Great," or "Big Jim," to distinguish him from "Little Jim," or James the Less, the son of Alphaeus, who was evidently a much smaller man. In our imagination we might picture James the Great as a large, corpulent man, huge of hand, piercing of eye, imposing, full-bearded, with a powerful resonant voice and an arresting, commanding, authoritative presence.

James was present at Pentecost, but we hear nothing more of him until his death some ten years later. What did James do during that interval? The Spanish have a long tradition that James introduced the Christian Faith to Spain. Associated with this is a rather farfetched legend that James, discouraged by the small numbers of converts, was comforted by a vision of the Virgin Mary on the banks of the Ebro River. (Mary, incidentally, was probably still living then.) Seated atop a pillar of jasper, surrounded by armies of angels, she appeared to him. James threw himself on his face before Mary, and she commanded him to build a chapel on that very spot so that people could venerate her there. The Spanish legend explains the origin of the Basilica of Our Lady of the Pillar at Saragossa. Afterward, the legend says, James returned to Jerusalem and was martyred there.

Some scholars think that the fact that James is not mentioned in Acts until his death is significant, and could indicate that the apostle was not in fact in Jerusalem much of the time. William S. McBirnie speculates that James went to preach to the Jewish colonists in Spain and annoyed Herod Agrippa, thus provoking Herod to have him murdered.[2] While this is conceivable, there is no firm tradition to this effect among the Church Fathers. When they mention him at all, they say that he was martyred in Jerusalem, but mention no travels in Spain or anywhere else.

James was put to death during the short reign of Herod Agrippa, probably in the year A.D. 42. Luke states that "King Herod started to harass some of the members of the Church. He beheaded James, the brother of John, and when he saw this pleased certain of the Jews, he took Peter into custody too." (Acts 12:1-3) Clement of Alexandria provides some further details about James' death. James, it seems, was tried before the members of the Sanhedrin, who condemned him for teaching that Christ was God and salvation was in Him alone. Herod approved the sentence and sentenced James to be beheaded. Normally, non-Roman citizens were executed by crucifixion. The fact that James was sentenced to die by the clean flash of the sword might indicate that he had somehow, sometime, obtained Roman citizenship. At any rate, the man who had denounced the apostle to the Sanhedrin was present at his trial, and was so moved that he declared himself a Christian. The Sanhedrin turned upon their former stooge and sentenced him to die along with James. As the two men walked side by side to the place of their execution, they were silent. Finally, the accuser asked James to forgive him. James continued silent for a minute, then turned, kissed him and said, "Peace be with you, brother."[3]

Whether or not James was actually in Spain, there is firmer ground to believe that his relics were eventually taken to northwest Spain, where they now repose in the famous Cathedral of St. James of Compostela. This was a great pilgrimage center during the Middle Ages and the site of hundreds of reported miracles. St. James became the patron of Spain and was invoked by the armies who drove the Moslems out of that country. According to some legends about Rodrigo Díaz de Vivar, the eleventh-century warrior known to history and literature as "El Cid" (The Conqueror), St. James appeared to him to lead him to victory over the infidel.

*   *   *

While we know only a little about James the Great, we know almost nothing about James the Less. There are hardly any traditions that have come down to us. Scripture states only that his father was Alphaeus and his mother Mary. In John's Gospel, one of the women at the cross, identified by Matthew and Mark as "Mary, the mother of James the Less and Joses," is here called "Mary, the wife of Cleopas." This does not contradict the lists of the apostles, which identify James as the son of Alphaeus, since both Alphaeus and Cleopas are Hellenizations of a Hebrew name most accurately transliterated as Halphai or Chalpai. This Cleopas, or Clopas, was one of the disciples to whom Jesus appeared on the road to Emmaus after His Resurrection. Hegesippus, a second-century Church historian, identified Cleopas as the brother of Joseph, the husband of the Virgin Mary.[4] Thus, legally, James would have been a first cousin of Jesus, but unlike James the Great, who was related on the maternal side, in this case there would have been no blood relation.

James the Less is not mentioned in the Scriptures except in the catalogues of the apostles. As with James the Great, the term "the Less" probably refers to size. We should not assume that he was less of a man than the son of Zebedee, or that he was an apostle of little consequence. He was probably called as he was because he was a little man.

We know that James had at least three brothers. One was St. Matthew, also identified as a son of Alphaeus. Another was Joses, about whom we know nothing. We know more about the third brother, Simeon, than we do about

James or even Matthew. Simeon became bishop of Jerusalem in A.D. 62, and moved the headquarters of the Church from Jerusalem to the town of Pella, where it survived the holocaust of A.D. 70 when Jerusalem was destroyed and its inhabitants massacred by the Romans. Eusebius states that Simeon reigned for about forty-five years until he was martyred under the Emperor Trajan around A.D. 107, when he was 120 years old. Quoting Hegesippus, Eusebius tells how Simeon was charged with being "a descendant of David and a Christian," and was executed by the governor Atticus. "Tortured for days on end, he bore a martyr's witness, so that all, including the governor, were astounded that at the age of 120 he could endure it; and he was ordered to be crucified."[5]

If Simeon was 120 in A.D. 107, he must have been born no later than 14 B.C. That would make him seven or eight years older than Jesus and in his mid-forties when the Lord was crucified. If Matthew and James were around the same age as Simeon, they would probably have been the oldest members of the apostolic college. We cannot assume this, however, since there may have been many more members of the family than the four brothers.

Of James the Less, we can say only that he was a son of Cleopas and Mary, and a brother of Simeon, Matthew and Joses, and that he was an apostle of Jesus Christ. Most scholars assume that he was born in Capernaum, since that is where his brother Matthew was working when he was called by Jesus. Some writers believe that, like Matthew, he was a tax collector before he was called. As to his career after Pentecost, we have hardly a clue. A modern writer named A.S. Atiya, in his *History of Eastern Christianity,* quoted by McBirnie, affirms certain old traditions that James was the first bishop of Syria. This would probably have placed him in Antioch. This does not harmonize with the *Constitution of the Holy Apostles* from the second century, which affirms that the first bishop of Antioch was Euodius, who was ordained by Peter. Other traditions state that James remained in Jerusalem and was stoned to death by a mob of irate Jews there. This is probably the better conclusion. It is possible that he remained in Jerusalem and under the shadow of his cousin, James the Righteous, and that he was killed in the same persecution of Christians in A.D. 62 that took the life of his better-known relative.

The fact that we know almost nothing about James the Less led the Rev. H.S. Vigeveno to call him the saint of the "nameless ones . . . named by the Savior and known by name to God,"[6] an inspiration for those who were discouraged by a lack of recognition and a reminder to such people that who they were and what they did was important to God.

* * *

The third James mentioned in the New Testament is by far the most important to Christian history. James the Righteous reigned as bishop of Jerusalem for more than thirty years, and interacted frequently with Peter and Paul.

The relationship of this James to Jesus is a problem. St. Paul identified James as "the brother of the Lord." (Gal. 1:19) Matthew and Mark list him as one of Jesus' "brothers and sisters." Hegesippus, too, refers to James as "the Lord's brother," and Eusebius states that he was Joseph's son. The commentators of the *New American Bible* write, "The question about the brothers of Jesus . . . cannot be easily decided on linguistic grounds. Greek-speaking Semites used the terms *adelphos* and *adelphe,* not only in the ordinary sense of blood brother and blood sister, but also for nephew, niece, half-brother, half-sister and cousin. The question of meaning here would not have arisen but for the faith of the [Roman Catholic] Church in Mary's perpetual virginity."

77

It should be pointed out that nearly all evangelical Protestants believe that James was a younger son of Mary and Joseph. Hegesippus, however, while stating that James was a son of Joseph, tells us that he was more than eighty when he was martyred in A.D. 62. This would have made him older than Jesus and thus a child of Joseph by a previous marriage. At least one apocryphal writer also holds this position. This would have made James a *stepbrother* of Jesus rather than a biological brother. However, there is nothing in Scripture itself that says Joseph had been married before his betrothal to Mary.

James was called "the Righteous" or "the Just" because of the scrupulous exactitude with which he attempted to practice the law of Moses. He had much in common with John the Baptist, and like many of the apostles, may have been a disciple of the Wilderness Prophet. Hegesippus has left us a vivid description of James. Holy from birth,

> he drank no wine or intoxicating liquor and ate no animal food; no razor came near his head; he did not smear himself with oil and took no baths. He alone was permitted to enter the holy place, for his garments were not of wool but of linen. He used to enter the sanctuary alone and was often found on his knees, beseeching forgiveness for the people, so that his knees grew hard like a camel's from his continually bending them in worship of God and beseeching forgiveness for the people. Because of his unsurpassable righteousness he was called the Righteous and . . . "Bulwark of the People."[7]

James was not a supporter of Jesus during his kinsman's earthly ministry. Like Paul, James in his zeal for the law was throwing the baby out with the bath. For a time he was blinded to the fact that no one could fully live up to the law. He did not understand (to quote the words of Father Augustus M. Toplady, the eighteenth-century British hymnist):

Not the labors of my hands
Can fulfill thy law's demands;
Could my zeal no respite know,
Could my tears for ever flow,
All for sin could not atone;
Thou must save, and Thou alone.

As in the case of Paul, it took a special Resurrection appearance to convince James that Jesus was Lord. As we shall see, however, James did not make as radical a change as Paul from the "doctrine of works" to the "doctrine of grace."

Immediately after the Ascension, James became one of the most important officers in the Church. Clement of Alexandria records that "Peter, James *the Great*, and John, after the Ascension of the Savior, did not claim preeminence because the Savior had specially honored them, but chose James the Righteous as the Bishop of Jerusalem."[8] He further states that along with Peter and John, James the Righteous was entrusted by the Risen Lord with "the higher knowledge" which they in turn imparted to the other apostles and the other apostles to the Seventy.[9]

Although not one of the Twelve, James, like Paul, had the authority of an apostle. In fact, his authority seems to have been greater than that of Paul or any other apostle except Peter and John. He is generally called the first bishop of Jerusalem. Actually, his precise position was the head of the elders, or "presbyters" — that is, the priests. He was also the spokesman for the Jewish wing of Christianity that prevailed in Jerusalem for many years.

It must be remembered that in the early days, members of the Christian Church in Palestine kept the Jewish law in its entirety. Children were circumcised, rules of ritual purification were observed, the Sabbath (sundown Friday to sundown Saturday) was kept as a day of rest, and Christians went to the temple for morning and afternoon prayers.[10] James was very much in favor of this. When he heard that his fellow convert Paul was telling gentile converts that they need not be circumcised or abide by the various rituals and regulations, he "hit the ceiling." At the Council of Jerusalem, James was persuaded by Peter to decree a policy for the universal Church that no irksome restrictions were to be imposed on gentile converts.

James, however, remained determined not to lose his Jewishness in embracing Christ, and insisted that all converts to Christianity from Judaism hold to the law in its entirety. This is why, even after the Council of Jerusalem, he attacked Peter at Antioch for "living like a gentile." Paul himself had to make concessions to the formidable bishop of Jerusalem. In A.D. 58, Paul arrived in Jerusalem and told James of his continuing success among the gentiles, only to have the crusty bishop point out that many of the Jewish Christians in Jerusalem were enraged by the fact that Paul was supposedly telling *Jewish* converts to "turn their backs on Moses" and forgo circumcision for their children. James called Paul on the carpet and ordered him "to do as we tell you." He ordered Paul to undergo the rite of purification so that "everyone will know that there is nothing in what they have been told about you, but that you follow the law yourself with due observance." (Acts 21:24) Paul did not argue. Nobody argued with James the Righteous. Paul obeyed.

One should not criticize James the Righteous as a man who was imperfectly converted. He sincerely wanted to conserve what was valuable in Judaism as well as embrace the "new way." He was also very much concerned about winning converts from the Jews of Jerusalem and also in preventing violent persecution. The Middle East was just as violent, and many of its citizens were just as unreasoning in the first, as in the twentieth century. After Paul complied with James' request to undergo the rite of purification, he was nearly lynched by a fanatical mob when he was seen in the temple. James was concerned that the lifestyle of Peter, Paul and other apostles who worked in other parts of the world, among more irenic people, not lead to pointless violence and aggression on the part of volatile, fanatical and belligerent inhabitants of Jerusalem and Palestine. By his continued zeal for the law, James was able to convert great numbers of Jews in Palestine. It may have been that circumcision and ritual purification were not essential for salvation, but these practices were so deeply ingrained in the souls of many in Jerusalem that their abandonment would have created a hopeless stumbling block. In this adherence to the law, James was really following the same principle proclaimed by Paul: to be "all things to all men," and not to be a cause of stumbling to others.

James' success in converting Jews brought about his death. This happened in Jerusalem in the spring of A.D. 62, after the death of the incumbent governor Festus, and before the appointment of his successor. A number of the "ruling class" of the Jews had gone over to Christianity, and the high priest Ananias was enraged with homicidal fury. The Sanhedrin summoned James. Interestingly enough, they looked to him to restrain the Christians. All seventy-one members of the council knew that there was no man in Jewry so zealous for the law as James. They also knew that he was at least sympathetic to Christianity. Moreover, they were aware that there had been friction between him and other Christian leaders over the observance of the law. Surely James did not go for this ridic-

81

ulous monkey business that Jesus was the Messiah. They might be willing to concede that He was a great man. Their predecessors had killed Him, but, well, that was "just one of those things," a lamentable error in judgment. But the insistence that this Jesus was not just a good man but the Son of God Almighty and Israel's Messiah was intolerable. Surely, so devout a Jew as James could not believe this humbug. He could call together the leaders of the Christian community and tell them, "Let's get this straight: Jesus was a great man and it is good to reverence his ethical teachings like those of any other famous rabbi, but let's not say that He was God." This is what the Sanhedrin expected James to do. According to Hegesippus, they told James to "make the facts about Jesus clear to all who come for Passover day. We all accept what you say: we can vouch for it, and so can all the people, that you are a righteous man and take no one at his face value. So make it clear to the crowd that they must not go astray as regards Jesus: the whole people and all of us accept what you say. So take your stand on the temple parapet, so that from that height you may be easily seen and your words audible to the whole people." Thus, thirty years almost to the day after Jesus was crucified, James was to make a public speech declaring the "true facts" about Jesus Christ.

On Passover, the courts of the temple were crowded with thousands of worshipers as James prepared to speak before the greatest audience of his life and tell them the "true facts" about Jesus. He climbed, apparently, to a walkway above one of the colonnades, where he could be seen and heard easily. The worshipers packed themselves in an immense throng before him. In the crowd were members of the Sanhedrin. When the crowd grew silent upon seeing this man, respected by Jew and Christian alike, about to speak, several members of the Sanhedrin shouted up to James, "Righteous One, whose word we are all obliged to accept, the people are going astray after Jesus who was crucified; so tell us what is meant by the 'Door of Jesus.'"

The answer that James proclaimed to the throng below was not the one that the Sanhedrin anticipated. "Why do you question me about the Son of Man?" he shouted. "I tell you, He is sitting in heaven at the right hand of the Great Power and He will come on the clouds of heaven!"

The crowd broke into cheers of "Hosanna to the Son of David!" and the members of the Sanhedrin, insane with fury, decided there and then to kill James so as to intimidate the crowd and prevent further conversions. Several of them rushed to the top of the parapet where James was speaking and threw him off onto the pavement below, where he was surrounded by a mob of local toughs who had accompanied the city fathers. As James lay stunned on the ground, they began to stone him. James began to pray, "I beseech Thee, Lord God and Father, forgive them. They do not know what they are doing."

Some of the crowd in the temple courts were horrified and began to shout, "Stop! What are you doing? The Righteous One is praying for you!" But they were unable to rescue James because of the mob which surrounded him. Some of James' attackers became ashamed and withdrew, but one brazen fellow, armed with something like a sledgehammer, took it and brought it down on James' head, killing him instantly.[11]

News of James' murder shocked most of Palestine, Jew, pagan and Christian alike. When the holy city was destroyed by the armies of Titus several years later, many attributed the overthrow of the city to God's wrath over the murder of the "Righteous One." With James' death, the Jewish Christianity that had insisted on the keeping of the entire law began to fade into oblivion.

James is usually considered the author of the Epistle of James, one of seven general, or "catholic," epistles in the New Testament. Eusebius writes, "Admittedly its authenticity is doubted, since few early writers refer to it . . . but the fact remains that . . . [it has] been regularly used in very many churches."[12]

The teaching in the Epistle of James is consistent with what we know from other sources about the redoubtable bishop of Jerusalem. James makes purity of conduct his chief concern. He writes:

If all you do is listen to it [the word], you are deceiving yourselves. A man who listens to God's word but does not put it into practice is like a man who looks into a mirror at the face he was born with: he looks at himself, then goes off and promptly forgets what he looked like. There is, on the other hand, the man who peers into freedom's ideal law and abides by it. He is not a forgetful listener, but one who carries out the law in practice. Blest will this man be in whatever he does. (Jas. 1:22-25)

Most famous are James' statements about the uselessness of lip service to the Christian profession without good works. "My brothers," he writes, "what good is it to profess faith without practicing it? Such faith has no power to save one, has it?" (Jas. 2:14) He goes on to say, "Do you believe that God is one? You are quite right. The demons believe that, and shudder. Do you want proof, you ignoramus, that without works faith is idle? Was not our father Abraham justified by his works when he offered his son Isaac on the altar? There you see proof that faith was both assisting his works and implemented by his works." (Jas. 2:19-22)

Finally, James' Epistle also furnishes scriptural grounds for the Sacrament of the Sick. He writes, "Is there anyone sick among you? He should ask for the presbyters of the church. They in turn are to pray over him, anointing him with oil in the Name [of the Lord]. This prayer uttered in faith will reclaim the one who is ill, and the Lord will restore him to health. If he has committed any sins, forgiveness will be his." (Jas. 5:14-16)

So the greatest of the three Jameses was not one of the Twelve. The Jewish Christianity for which he stood, though now extinct, should be remembered as a powerful force in the early Church. We cannot tell whether James the Great and James the Less were more in sympathy with him or with Peter and Paul, but it is interesting to note that all three men were martyred in Jerusalem.

5

John: The beloved thunderer

IF one of the polls questioned churchgoers as to which apostle they most admired, the winner, hands down, would almost certainly be John. Whereas Peter has been criticized for his apparent inconstancy and the various *faux pas* recorded of him in Scripture, and most of the other apostles have been written off as thickheaded, uncomprehending dolts, John has been praised as "The Apostle of Love," the paragon of "angelic virtue" and unparalleled devotion. Philip Schaff described him as "a man of mystic contemplation . . . simple, serene, profound, intuitive, sublime. . . ."[1] It is frequently pointed out that it was he who was closest to the Lord, that it was he who best understood Christ's teaching. Alone, out of all the male disciples, it was he who stood at the foot of the cross, comforting Our Lady. St. John is usually portrayed as a frail, androgynous, ethereal-looking youth or an angelic-looking patriarch, gaunt and white-bearded, lost in contemplation. If most Christians were asked to give words they thought best applied to John, common responses would be: peace, love, gentleness, kindness, spirituality, purity, piety and holiness. Yet many forget that Jesus' surname for John was "Son of Thunder" — Thunderson — and that much of the material that has survived about John reveal anything but the Caspar Milquetoast apostle that he is popularly believed to have been.

What does the Bible tell us about Johanan bar Zebedee? First of all, we know that he was a brother of James the Great and a son of Zebedee and Salome. His life-dates are much easier to approximate than those of most of the other apostles. It is fairly certain that John died in A.D 100 (give or take a year) and that he was over ninety. *The Apostolic History of Abdias* states that he was exactly ninety-seven, which is not unreasonable. That would give John a birth year in approximately A.D. 3. Thus, he was in his mid-twenties when called by Jesus.

Of John's early life we know little, except that he was probably from Bethsaida and worked for his father in the fishing business. Like Peter, Andrew and his brother James, John almost certainly had some education and was literate. Like them, he was almost certainly familiar with the Greek culture and language, but was a devout and zeal-ous Jew. It is likely that he was, like Peter, Andrew and James, a disciple of John the Baptist. It may very well be that "the other disciple" who was with Andrew when the Baptist pointed out Jesus as "the Lamb of God" was John. Like Andrew, John never married. In fact, St. Augustine writes that from earliest youth, John cultivated "singular chastity."[2]

Like all the other apostles except Peter, John is men-tioned infrequently in the Gospels, and usually only in passing. He was, with his brother and Peter, part of the "inner circle." Jesus sent him along with Peter to make preparations for the Last Supper. He seems to have had no better comprehension of Jesus' ministry than the other apostles. Jesus had to scold him for jockeying for an im-portant post in the new Israeli government he imagined was imminent. As we have seen, he was reproved when he asked Jesus to destroy a village where they had been treated rudely. Jesus also corrected John when the apostle suggested that a man who was driving out demons in

Jesus' name should be stopped. Jesus told John that the man who was not against Him was in fact for Him, and was not to be hindered. "No man who performs a miracle using my name can at the same time speak ill of me." (Mk. 9:39)

In the Gospel of John, St. John is probably to be identified with "the disciple whom Jesus loved," and who, at the Last Supper, lay with his head on Jesus' breast. There are two possible explanations of the term "the disciple whom Jesus loved" that hold water. The first assumes that the expression originated with John, who used it out of modesty. Several times in his Gospel he refers to "another disciple" and "the other disciple." Since John assumes all his readers knew that all the apostles were beloved by Jesus, the term "the disciple whom Jesus loved" is simply a synonym for "disciple" and a device to permit the author to avoid using "I" or his own name. Others, pointing out that John's Gospel was likely published by an editor after the apostle's death, feel that the editor used the term in homage to John, as if to imply that of all the apostles, his master was the one who was closest to Jesus.

The "disciple whom Jesus loved" appears at the Last Supper. A literal translation of the Greek states that he was leaning on Jesus' breast. (Jn. 13:23) Some twentieth-century people have looked askance at this. In those days, however, it was customary for guests to recline side by side in such a way that the head of one guest was parallel to the chest of the person next to him. If one wished to speak privately to that person, one would move close enough so that one's head was nearly or actually resting on the neighbor's chest. This is what happened at the Last Supper, when John was reclining between Peter and Jesus, who was in turn between Judas and John. Jesus had just announced that one of His apostles would betray Him. Peter, who was apparently on John's left, with his head at

John's chest, bade him ask Jesus to identify the traitor. John then leaned back so that his head was against Jesus' chest as he asked Him to privately disclose who it was who would betray Him. Jesus took a piece of bread and told John that the man to whom He gave the morsel was the man to watch. He then gave it to Judas, who was on the other side of him and thus unable to follow Jesus' conversation with John.

We next hear of John, along with Peter and James, at Gethsemane. John does not record the fact, reported by Matthew and Mark, that he and his colleagues were unable to keep awake. In fact, John does not speak of what took place in Gethsemane before the arrest. After that, he and Peter followed Jesus to the palace of the high priest and were admitted into the courtyard where they could overhear the travesty of a trial to which the Lord was subjected. John, who was known to the family of the high priest through business dealings, was probably instantly recognized as one of Jesus' disciples. Apparently he made no fuss about it, despite the disconcerting behavior of his friend Peter, who thrice denied that he was a disciple and then rushed from the courtyard in tears at the crowing of the cock.

Peter was apparently too ashamed and grief-stricken to witness the Crucifixion. Out of all the Twelve, John alone was there, along with his mother, his aunt (Jesus' Mother), his aunt by marriage (Mary, the wife of Cleopas), and the female disciple Mary of Magdala, or Mary Magdalene. It was there at the cross that Jesus entrusted His Mother into John's care.

Why did Jesus do this? Is this not an argument against the existence of any real brothers and sisters? This is not necessarily the case. Mary was only about fifty and doubtless quite able to make her own choices and to take care of herself. We should remember that John was a bachelor and probably lived with his parents and that his mother was Mary's sister. It is certainly not remarkable for a widow to opt to live with her sister. Moreover, it is possible that no one was capable of providing for Mary as comfortably as could her nephew John. From that day on, John tells us that the Virgin Mary lived in his household.

John was one of the first disciples aware of the Resurrection. The empty tomb had been discovered first by three women: John's mother, Mary Magdalene and Mary, the wife of Cleopas. Even though they had been favored with an angelic vision, Mary Magdalene was still not convinced and ran to Peter and John to report the theft of the Master's body. Even a vision is not always sufficient to convince some people of the fracture of what they perceive to be the laws of nature. John's account of the hurried trip to the tomb betrays certain autobiographical touches, such as the fact that he outran Peter but waited outside the tomb while his friend went in. He recounts that he then went in and "saw and believed." (Jn. 20:8) This is John's way of saying, "This is when I became convinced of the Resurrection."

The Fourth Gospel recounts several Resurrection experiences, including the instance in which Peter demanded to know what would happen to John. Jesus' response, "Suppose I want him to stay until I come, how does that concern you? Your business is to follow me," (Jn. 21:22) led some people to assume that John would never die. John, or his editor, took pains to explain that this statement was simply Jesus' way of telling Peter to mind his own business.

John is mentioned only occasionally after Pentecost. Paul speaks of him as being, with Peter and James the Righteous, one of the "pillars" of the Church. (Gal. 2:9) John was instrumental in the healing of the cripple at the beautiful gate of the temple, mentioned briefly in our second chapter on Peter. Luke tells us how at 3 p.m. John and Peter were on their way to the temple to pray and were solicited for alms by a crippled beggar at one of the temple gates. "I have neither silver nor gold," said Peter, "but what I have I give you! In the name of Jesus Christ the Nazorean, walk!" (Acts 3:6) Peter helped the beggar to his feet and the man immediately astounded all onlookers to whom he had become a familiar fixture by not only walking, but running and leaping. As we have seen, this healing was the occasion for the apostles' arrest and for a hearing before the Sanhedrin, in which they were forbidden to teach in Jesus' name. As we know, the Twelve did not keep this promise.

We hear of John once more in Acts, when he and Peter journeyed to Samaria to lay hands upon the converts there. Although most of the apostles seem to have left Jerusalem after the martyrdom of John's brother James, John apparently was still living there in A.D. 49, at the time of the Council of Jerusalem.

Indeed, John seems to have been one of the least-traveled of the Twelve. Perhaps this was because of his responsibility towards his parents and his aunt. He traveled around Palestine with Peter, visiting the various communities there, but seems to have remained in Jerusalem long after Peter left. F.M. Braun, author of *Jean le theologian*, felt that John was very close to James the Righteous doctrinally, and was "intent on renouncing as little as possible of authentic Judaism."[3] Cardinal Danielou concurs, pointing out that in Revelation, John sharply condemned Christians who ate meat sacrificed to pagan deities, while Paul, in I Corinthians, took a much more lenient position.[4] So John likely remained in Jerusalem until the A.D. 60s. It was perhaps after the death of James the Righteous that John left Jerusalem and headed for Rome, where he was reunited with his great friend Peter.

Both Tertullian and Jerome stated that John was nearly martyred at Rome, that he was thrown into a cauldron of hot oil, but somehow emerged unhurt. It is possible that when the Neronian persecution broke out, John was imprisoned and tortured, but somehow escaped and made his way to Ephesus to take over the "orphaned" churches of Asia, once superintended by the martyred Paul. This would have been around A.D. 66 or 67.

Asia in those days was not identified with the vast continent that we call by that name today, but with the extreme west coast of modern Turkey, on the Aegean Sea. Ephesus, then the abode of about 250,000 people, was a wealthy city and one of the most important ports on the Aegean. It was famed for its huge temple to Artemis, which was considered one of the Seven Wonders of the World. Ephesus also sported a gymnasium, a stadium, a library and an immense theater with seating for 24,000. A magnificent colonnaded avenue, known as the Arcadian Way, ran from the harbor to the great theater. The people of Ephesus included a number of Jews as well as a Christian community which had been founded before Paul's first visit.

John seems to have made his home in Ephesus for the rest of his life. There he supervised all the Christian churches in the province of Asia. These included Smyrna, which was a large commercial center; Pergamum, the center of the parchment-manufacturing industry; Thyatira, the center of the purple-dye industry; and Sardis, Philadelphia and Laodicea, all cities once prosperous but then in decline after an immense earthquake that ravaged them in A.D. 17. These were the churches which John mentioned in Revelation. According to *The Constitutions of the Holy Apostles,* John ordained bishops as well as priests in each of those cities.

The date and place of the death of the Virgin Mary are

debatable. Since the fourth century, there was a very strong tradition that she went with John to Ephesus and died there. There stands a building which for many years has been identified as her house. Inasmuch as John probably did not settle in Ephesus until A.D. 66 at the earliest, this would have made Mary at least ninety at the time, and it would be hard to imagine a woman of that age surviving persecution, torture and imprisonment in Rome, fleeing into the countryside and traveling long distances under adverse conditions. The earlier tradition that Mary died in Jerusalem in John's house on Mount Zion is perhaps more reliable. There is a structure still extant in Jerusalem which has a long tradition as Mary's tomb. According to this tradition, it was from there that the Virgin's body was assumed, incorrupt, into heaven.

There are five writings in the New Testament attributed to John: the Fourth Gospel, the Revelation and three epistles. There was no serious doubt by the early Church Fathers that the Gospel and the first epistle had been written by John. The second and third epistles, Eusebius thought, might have been the work of a man named John the Presbyter, who was ordained by the apostle John and who succeeded him as bishop of Ephesus. Cyril of Jerusalem, John Chrysostom and Gregory Nazianzus felt that Revelation, too, was from the hand of John the Presbyter. However, the weight of ancient opinion, in the writings of Justin Martyr, Irenaeus, Clement of Alexandria and Tertullian, hold that the Apocalypse is the work of the apostle John.

Eusebius tells us about the composition of John's Gospel:

And when Mark and Luke had now published their gospels, John, we are told, who hitherto had relied entirely on the spoken word, finally took to writing for the following reason. The three gospels already written were in general circulation and copies had come into John's hands. He welcomed them, we are told, and confirmed their accuracy, but remarked that the narrative only lacked the story of what Christ had done first of all at the beginning of His mission.

This tradition is undoubtedly true. Anyone can see that the three evangelists have recorded the doings of the Savior for only one year, following the consignment of John the Baptist to prison, and that they indicated this very fact at the beginning of their narrative. After the forty days' fast and the temptation that followed, Matthew shows clearly the period covered by his narrative when he says: "Hearing that John had been arrested, He withdrew from Judaea into Galilee. . . ."

We are told, then, for this reason the apostle John was urged to record in his gospel the period which the earlier evangelists passed over in silence and the things done during that period by the Savior. . . .Once this is grasped, there no longer appears to be a discrepancy between the gospels, because John's deals with the early stages of Christ's career and the others cover the last period of His story. . . .[5]

Clement of Alexandria called John's Gospel the "spiritual Gospel" because it is the most doctrinal and theological of the four. John seems to take pains to present Jesus' theological teaching in greater detail than the other evangelists, and intersperses his own comment in the narrative. Because John's Gospel is the most theological, John is sometimes called "St. John the Divine," which, in Jacobean English, means "the Theologian."

Most scholars feel that John's Gospel was written in a painstaking manner. It is possible that the book took many years to complete. It was written in Greek for gentile believers. It shows a number of autobiographical touches, such as the fact that John outran Peter to the tomb and the fact that he saw an issue of water and blood from the riven side of Christ. Still, there is internal evidence that the Fourth Gospel was put into its *final* form by an editor after John's death. The Gospel concludes with the words, "It is this same disciple who is the witness to these things; it is he who wrote them down and his testimony, we know, is true." (Jn. 21:24) It is possible that John toiled on his Gospel for years and that it was released only after his death, when it was prepared for publication by his disciples at Ephesus.

Some commentators think that "John was just a little bit too old" when he wrote his first epistle, an encyclical letter for the churches under his supervision. They claim to find no "logical arrangement" or "progression of thought," merely sentences strung together in a rambling way with no real order. Even so, in it John answers effectively the question "How do I know that I am in Christ?" The answer to this is that if we keep Christ's commandments, give our allegiance to Christ and love each other — all results of the indwelling of the Holy Spirit — we know that we are in Christ. John tells us that we can be confident that Christ will keep us from sin and that eternal life is to know and understand Christ.

John makes some severe statements, too. He tells his readers that the man who deliberately sins is a child of the devil. (I Jn. 3:8) He tells us that "the man who says, 'I know him,' while he disobeys His commands, is a liar." (I Jn. 2:5, NEB) These statements give some clue as to why John was surnamed "Son of Thunder." Although his attitude is basically loving and gentle, he states in no uncertain terms the fact that mere lip service to Christianity does not make for salvation. In his Gospel, John includes a number of hell-and-damnation quotations from Jesus, such as the passage in which Jesus tells His detractors that they are children not of Abraham but of the devil and will die in their sins unless they believe in Him. (Jn. 8:40ff) John was not a man who was afraid to mention God's threats along with His promises. To the receptive he could be the "Apostle of Love," but to the unrepentant "The Son of Thunder."

In A.D. 81 the Emperor Domitian came to power. He began his official letters referring to himself as "Our Lord and God." He ordered his subjects to address him as a god and commanded that gold and silver statues of himself be erected in the pagan temples.[6] He did not take kindly to Christianity, and began another persecution, in which St. Philip ultimately lost his life. Once again John escaped death, but he was exiled to a prison colony on a small Aegean island called Patmos. It was here, suffering "because I proclaimed God's word and bore witness to Jesus," (Rev. 1:9) one Sunday that John was "caught up in ecstasy" and favored with a vision which became the basis for the book known as the Apocalypse and the Revelation. Over the years there have been almost as many interpretations of this book as there have been readers. Luther was rather negative toward it because he found it obscure, and "a revelation should be revealing."[7] Other writers have expressed the opinion that if any part of Revelation is not plain, it is because God wanted it that way. Although John prepared the Revelation to show "what must happen very soon," (Rev.1:1) he surely did not mean for his work to be taken as an almanac of specific predictions. Certain modern evangelical authors claim to derive from it the most exact predictions about the behavior of such modern nations as Israel, the Soviet Union and China, and even a timetable for the events of the "end time." Nearly all the early Church Fathers who wrote about Revelation interpreted it in a much more mystical and allegorical way. John wrote the Apocalypse not as a history or as a doctrine, to be taken straightforwardly as his Gospel and epistle, but as a revelation of things that are beyond the full comprehension of the human intellect, which can be understood imperfectly only through a symbol or a figure. To interpret Revelation with the gross and wooden literalism of some modern evangelicals would be an improper interpretation.

On September 18, A.D. 96, there was a coup with the result that Domitian was overthrown and slain, and a senator by the name of Marcus Cocceius Nerva became emperor. The first in a succession of rulers known as "The Good Emperors," Nerva did not persecute the Church and allowed John to return to Ephesus. Although the apostle was now about ninety-three, he immediately set out to reorganize and invigorate his churches. Clement of Alexandria tells us that the old man traveled extensively through his territories, organizing new churches, appointing bishops and ordaining men who were "pointed out by the Spirit."[8] Several future leaders of the Church, including Papias and Polycarp, studied under John during the waning years of the first century.

Clement recounted "a true account" which illustrated the character of the ancient John. While in Smyrna to mediate a dispute, John left a young convert in the care of the newly appointed bishop, who was to supervise the youth's spiritual training. After the convert was baptized, the bishop lost track of him and the next thing anyone knew, the young man had fallen into bad company and taken to crime. Moving from "petty offenses" to major crime, he became the leader of a band of thugs, notorious for their "violence, cruelty, and blood-thirstiness."

When John returned to Smyrna he inquired about the convert. The embarrassed bishop said, "The boy is dead." "Dead?" asked John. "How did he die?" Then the bishop was forced to tell him that the young man was now the leader of a gang of highwaymen. The old apostle tore his clothing in the Middle Eastern gesture of mourning, and let the thunderbolt of his wrath fall upon the bishop who had been so careless as to neglect to supervise his recent converts. Despite his four score and fifteen years, John called for a horse and galloped off for the backcountry where the former convert was believed to be hiding out with his cohorts. Presently, he was surrounded by members of the gang. "I'm not going to try to escape and I ask for no mercy," said John. "This is what I have come for. Now, take me to your leader."

When the bandit chief saw John, he turned and ran. "Why are you running away from me, my boy?" said John, puffing after him. "Why are you running from your own father, who is unarmed and very old? Be sorry for me, child, not afraid of me. You still have hopes of life. I will account to Christ for you. If need be, I will gladly suffer your death, as the Lord suffered death for us. To save you I will give my own life. Stop! Believe! Christ sent me!"

The chief, who could have easily eluded the old man, halted and approached John and fixed his eyes on the ground. The apostle moved toward him and the bandit flung his arms about him, sobbing, while John knelt and kissed the young man's right hand as a token that the member with which he had wielded his sword had now been cleansed by repentance. And so John led the young man back to Smyrna and, in Clement's words, "interceded for him with many prayers, shared with him the ordeal of continuous fasting, brought his mind under control by all the enchanting power of his words, and did not leave him . . . till he had restored him to the Church."[9]

In the early Church, if a person committed a mortal sin, he was admitted back to fellowship only after a long and rigorous period of penance. John insisted on this. We also see his great compassion and concern. He saw everyone in his flock as an individual, worthy of his personal concern and was harshly disposed to bishops who did not feel similarly. When he learned that one convert had "backslidden," he risked his health and safety to personally intercede with the man. Surely, John was a man who tempered thunder with love.

Polycarp recounted to Irenaeus another story that illustrates John's character. One day John, Polycarp and some other friends entered a bathhouse (most houses did not have indoor plumbing then) and plunged into the waters. They had not been there long when there entered the baths a man named Cerinthus, a preacher who denied Christ's divinity and advocated self-indulgence and sensual luxuries. When John saw him he "leapt from the spot and ran for the door," crying to his companions, "Let's get out of here before the place falls in, now that Cerinthus, the enemy of truth, is inside."[10] While compassionate to the penitent, John would not even share the same public facilities with someone who knowingly and deliberately perverted the truth.

The fifth-century writer Cassian gives us another vignette into John's character. Someone found the apostle playing with a partridge and expressed his surprise at seeing such an eminent and august man doing something so trivial as playing with a bird. "Don't take offense at this brief and silent relaxation of mine," John told him. "If I didn't get the opportunity to relax like this once in a while, I would collapse from overwork and not be able to fulfill my duties."[11]

An "orthodox writer" named Apollonius (A.D. 150-220), who may have known people who knew John, wrote that John's ministry was attended by many miracles and that he had even raised a dead man in Ephesus in his later years.[12] Polycrates (A.D. 126-200), a later bishop of Ephesus, recorded that John always insisted that Easter be celebrated on the actual anniversary of Jesus' Resurrection, regardless of the day of the week on which it fell.[13]

Eusebius, Irenaeus and Clement of Alexandria all stated that John lived into the reign of Trajan, which began in January, A.D. 98. According to Jerome, he finally was overtaken by a crippling illness. Even then he insisted on being literally carried into the church in the arms of his disciples and taken to the front of the congregation where he managed to say, "Little children, love one another." Some of his disciples asked him why he went to such trouble when he had so little to say. "It is the Lord's command, and if this alone is done, it is enough."[14]

When death drew near, John directed that his disciples dig his grave outside the city limits. As the sun was setting one evening, he asked to be carried to his grave. Signing himself with the cross, he prayed, "Be Thou with me, Lord Jesus Christ." He gazed at his disciples and said, "Peace be with you, my brethren," and went to be with the Lord.[15]

6

Philip:
First evangelist
to the gentiles

PHILIP, a native of Bethsaida, was probably a lifelong friend of Peter, Andrew, James and John and, like them, a fisherman. According to some traditions, he belonged to the tribe of Zebulun. Like many first-century Galilean Jews, he had a Greek name. "Philip," which means "horse-lover," became especially popular after 4 B.C., when the son of Herod the Great who bore that name became Tetrarch of Ituraea, Gaulanitis and Trachonitis (the territories adjoining Galilee).

Philip is mentioned only by name, as one of the Twelve, by Matthew, Mark and Luke. John made four references to him. The first was in the opening chapter of his Gospel. From this passage it seems clear that Philip, like his colleagues from Galilee, was first a disciple of John the Baptist. Along with his friends he met Jesus at Bethabara, and shortly afterward introduced his friend Nathanael to the man he described as "the one Moses spoke of in the law." (Jn. 1:45)

We meet Philip again in the sixth chapter of John, at the feeding of the five thousand. John tells us that in order to "test" Philip, Jesus asked, "Where shall we buy bread for these people to eat?" (Jn. 6:5) Philip's reaction was

101

entirely practical and human. He told Jesus that he had only two hundred denarii (the equivalent of perhaps forty dollars) and this, of course, would not buy enough loaves so that each person could get even a mouthful. Here Philip's role ends, as we are told that he was interrupted by Andrew, who told Jesus of the boy with the loaves and fishes. If this incident cast any light on Philip's character, it was perhaps to contrast his response to Andrew's. Philip, in this instance, saw only the human impossibility of buying dinner for the equivalent of a football stadium full of people with only forty dollars. Andrew looked beyond the limitations of money and human ingenuity to the all-sufficient power of Jesus.

Again we hear of Philip in conjunction with Andrew, just before the Crucifixion. Approached by Greek pagans who wished to speak with Jesus, Philip was seemingly undecided as to what he should do and conferred with his friend Andrew before introducing the inquirers to Jesus. Here again it would seem that Andrew's understanding of Jesus is contrasted unfavorably with Philip's. It would seem that this incident revealed Philip's doubts as to whether Jesus had come to save anyone except Jews, and subsequently showed his hesitation as to whether to trouble his Master with gentile inquirers. Andrew here showed a better perception of the universality of Jesus' mission, as he convinced Philip that the Greeks should in fact be taken to Jesus. (Jn. 12:20-26)

The last incident in which Philip was mentioned really told us almost nothing about him. We are told that he interrupted Jesus while He was teaching. "If you really knew me, you would know my Father also," the Master said. "From this point on you know him; you have seen him." (Jn. 14:7) At this point Philip broke in. "Lord, show us the Father and that will be enough for us." Jesus' reply was, "Philip, after I have been with you all this time, you

102

still do not know me?" (Jn. 14:8-9) Someone might be moved to comment, "This Philip was a stupid man. He did not understand that the Lord could meet all his needs. He did not comprehend that Jesus had come to save the world. And, after studying with Him three years, Philip was seemingly unaware that Jesus was God. Why would the Lord have chosen such an uncomprehending man?"

It is true that Philip apparently did not fully comprehend Jesus' divinity before the Resurrection. We must remember, however, that this was a radically new and alien concept even for the most devout and scholarly Jew — that the Messiah was fully man and fully God and had come to suffer and die. We must recall that Philip, in the face of incomprehension, did the right thing. He asked for clarification. Instead of nursing doubts and contradictions and permitting them to grow, Philip went to the One who could resolve them.

We hear no more of Philip in the Bible, except that he was part of the group that met, after Jesus' Ascension, in the upper room in Jerusalem. There are, however, a number of references to a man named Philip in Acts, but there is considerable doubt as to whether they refer to Philip the apostle. In the sixth chapter, Luke names the men who were set aside as "deacons" by the apostles: Stephen, Philip, Prochorus, Nicanor, Timon, Parmenas and Nicolaus. As to the identity of the man called Philip the deacon and later Philip the evangelist, no one can be absolutely certain. The Twelve complained that administrative concerns were causing them to neglect the preaching of God's Word, and thus they appointed the deacons to assist them. If Philip the apostle and Philip the deacon were the same man, we must assume that he was a man of such energy that he was willing to undertake responsibilities and a workload that the rest of his colleagues considered intolerable.

However, most of the early Church Fathers insisted that Philip the apostle and Philip the deacon were the same man. Eusebius, Polycarp, Irenaeus, Polycrates and Tertullian all said this. Since the college of deacons served the Hellenistic wing of the Church, it was conceivable that the Twelve felt that one of their number should be a part of that body, so as to ensure orthodoxy. Since the Hellenists were the first to reach the gentiles, Philip's ministry would have been directed to non-Jews earlier than that of any of his colleagues.

Philip left Jerusalem for Samaria in A.D. 36, after the death of Stephen. Samaria lay north of Judea and south of Galilee. Philip immediately began to proclaim to the people that Jesus was the Messiah, not only for the Jews, but for them. This message was greeted by crowds which grew progressively larger and more enthusiastic, especially when a number of miracles took place. Luke recorded that "there were many who had unclean spirits, which came out shrieking loudly. Many others were paralytics or cripples, and these were cured. The rejoicing in that town rose to fever pitch." (Acts 8:7-8)

Philip also had an encounter with Simon Magus, the same warlock who tried to buy the Holy Spirit from St. Peter. When many of his disciples were converted, Simon too professed conversion and was even baptized, and "became a devoted follower of Philip. He watched the signs and the great miracles as they occurred, and was quite carried away." (Acts 8:13)

This lasted only until Peter and John arrived. After they prayed for the baptism of the Spirit, Simon Magus offered them money for the ability to summon the Spirit. Peter immediately recognized that Simon's conversion was only a sham to keep from losing his followers.

This incident seemed to illustrate the primacy of Peter and John among the Twelve. After Philip did his evangelical work, the other two apostles made a visitation, tying up what were apparently loose ends in his ministry there. Obviously, Philip had neglected to pray for the baptism of his converts in the Holy Spirit, and he had also failed to recognize that he was being "had" by a local cultist. We see here the concern of Peter and other apostles for unity in the Faith. Morton Smith, professor of ancient history at Columbia University, wrote of the "widely different Gospels" preached by the missionaries of the apostolic age.[1] British scholar Paul Johnson wrote of "a babel of voices"[2] that characterized the early Church. Still, the New Testament bears witness, on the contrary, to the unity of one catholic (that is, universal) faith taught and maintained in an orderly manner by the apostles.

Moving south, Philip headed for the city of Gaza, which lay on the coast, approximately forty-five miles southwest of Jerusalem. While only a few miles outside the holy city, he encountered on the highway the carriage of the Ethiopian minister of finance. Most translations spoke of a "chariot," which is generally thought of as a small two-wheeled vehicle. The Ethiopian statesman was, however, most likely traveling in an open, four-wheeled carriage, generally favored in interurban travel in those days.

Ethiopia, then called Axum, was a powerful kingdom independent of Rome. Eusebius tells us that in the first century it was ruled by women. Like most nations of antiquity (including Rome) the royal palaces abounded in castrated slaves, many of whom were promoted to positions of power and wealth. The finance minister whom Philip encountered was in that unhappy physical state.

The minister was also a Jew. For millennia, Ethiopia had a substantial population of black Jews. The country's last Christian ruler, Haile Selassie I, overthrown by the communists in 1974, claimed descent from Solomon and the Queen of Sheba. The queen's finance minister was, in fact, on his way home from a pilgrimage to Jerusalem.

Philip heard the voice of God telling him to overtake the carriage. The highway was evidently crowded and the carriage was lumbering slowly enough for Philip to overtake it on foot. As he drew alongside he overheard the minister reading the fifty-third chapter of Isaiah: "Like a sheep he was led to the slaughter, like a lamb before its shearer he was silent and opened not his mouth. In his humiliation he was deprived of justice. Who will ever speak of his posterity, for he is deprived of his life on earth?" In those days, people tended to read aloud rather than silently. Philip asked the Ethiopian if he understood what he was reading. The official said he did not, and invited Philip to climb up into the carriage and explain it to him. So Philip had the opportunity to show the minister how the passage in question referred to Christ. Converted and baptized at a creek by the road, the royal finance minister returned to Axum to spread the Gospel there. To this day the Ethiopian Orthodox Church traces its episcopal succession back to St. Philip, who, they insist, ordained the finance minister a bishop.

After he baptized the minister, Philip suddenly disappeared. "The Spirit of the Lord snatched Philip away and the eunuch saw him no more." (Acts 8:39) Philip found himself at Azotus, a town some thirty miles away, where he "went about announcing the good news in all the towns until he reached Caesarea." (Acts 8:40) Here was an apparent instance of bilocation, that is, the phenomenon whereby an individual appears to be in two places at once. This was observed often in modern times in the Italian priest, Padre Pio Forgione (1887-1968). Typically, Pio, who for the last fifty years of his life never left the city where his friary was located, went into a trance and appeared to speak to unseen persons. At the same time, in another part of Italy — even of the world — he was seen and spoken to. Padre Pio often spoke of the phenomenon as a projection of his personality. Perhaps Philip was "really" at Azotus when he was projected by the Spirit to meet the carriage of the Ethiopian official.

Luke wrote that Philip, after preaching in a number of towns in Palestine, went to Caesarea. For more than twenty years he made his home there. We are told that in A.D. 58 Paul and Luke, en route to Jerusalem, visited him and his family there. Luke noted that Philip had four unmarried daughters, all of whom possessed the gift of prophecy. Shortly after that Paul, as he had himself anticipated, was arrested. Emil Kraeling, for many years professor at Union Theological Seminary in New York, speculated that Paul, on his visit, may have requested Philip to take over some of his churches in Asia if anything happened to him. Shortly after Paul's arrest in Jerusalem, Philip and his family moved to the city of Hierapolis in Asia Minor. Hierapolis, which means "Holy City" in Greek, was the site of a famous chemical spring which sparkled out of the rocks and cascaded over the mountainside in falls almost as large as Niagara.³ It was a resort city that attracted the truly sick as well as the hypochondriac from all over the Near and Middle East. There is very good evidence for Philip's residence here.

Eusebius, quoting a letter from Polycrates written around A.D. 185, points out: "In Asia great luminaries sleep who shall rise again on the last day, the day of the Lord's advent, when he is coming with glory from heaven and shall search out all His saints — such as Philip, one of the twelve Apostles, who sleeps in Hierapolis with two of his daughters, who remained unmarried to the end of their days, while the other daughter lived in the Holy Spirit and rests in Ephesus."⁴ Eusebius also cites the writer Gaius (A.D. 160-230), who wrote, "There were four prophetesses in Hierapolis in Asia, daughters of Philip. Their grave is there, as is their father's."[5]

Philip evidently supervised the churches in the area of Asia Minor known as Phrygia, just as John would eventually supervise the area directly to the west, known as Asia. In his duties Philip was assisted by his sister Miriam, for a time by St. Bartholomew, and later by his daughters.

Many of the uneducated people in Hierapolis were devotees of the unwholesome cult of Echidna, which involved snake worship. A fourth-century novel, called *The Acts of Philip,* gives a fanciful account of how Philip went up to the altar of the god and commanded the sacred serpent to depart in the Name of Christ, and how the loathsome reptile glided from beneath the altar, "emitting such a hideous stench that many of the people died, and among them, the king's son fell dead in the arms of his attendants: but the Apostle, by divine power, restored him to life."[6] Obviously, there is quite a bit of fabrication here, but it is conceivable that just as St. Boniface would later chop down a tree held sacred by Germanic pagans, St. Philip, to demonstrate to the heathen that no evil would befall him by such an act, released one or more sacred serpents. It is also a fact that one of Philip's daughters told Polycrates that her father did in fact raise a man from the dead at Hierapolis, but went into no details.[7]

While based in Hierapolis, Philip made several missionary trips. Isidore of Seville (A.D. 560-636), the Spanish author, maintained that the apostle preached in France, but he confused *Gallia* (France) with *Galatia,* an area of Asia Minor where Philip really did preach. It is also believed that Philip preached in Carthage, in what is now Tunisia. Aboard ship a Jew named Hananiah ridiculed him and insisted that Jesus "has become dust and lies in Jerusalem while you lead ignorant men astray by his name."

After Philip saved Hananiah's life in a storm, however, the Jew was converted and baptized.

When Philip arrived in Carthage, he began to preach to the pagans there, bidding them, "Trust in God and be glad. Believe, my dear ones, for He will forgive your sins when you turn to Him with all your heart, with a pure mind free of doubt." Philip received an enthusiastic response, and before he returned to Hierapolis after an extended stay in Carthage, he had baptized 3,000 gentiles and 1,500 Jews.[8]

Philip was evidently a widower by the time he went to Hierapolis, but his four daughters were prominent in the life of the Church during the first and early second centuries. An ancient Greek litany of saints identified them as Hermione, Chariline, Irais and Eutychiane.[9] All of them had lived to be very old. One of them had married; another "lived in the Spirit" at Ephesus; and the other two had died unmarried at Hierapolis.[10] All were known as prophetesses, but the oldest sister, Hermione, who was martyred during the reign of Hadrian (A.D. 117-138), was also renowned for her gift of healing.[11] All were evidently important Church leaders. The youngest, Eutychiane, lived to be more than a hundred years old, since Polycrates knew her in the middle of the second century.

Philip lost his life at the age of eighty-seven, probably around A.D. 90, during the persecutions of Dominian. He had attracted the ire of the Roman governor (Hierapolis did not have a king, as claimed in the *Acts of Philip*) when his wife was cured of an eye disease through the prayers of the apostle. The old man was, like Peter, crucified upside down. His last words were, "Clothe me in Thy glorious robe and the seal of Thy light that ever shineth, until I have passed by all the rulers of the world and the evil dragon that opposeth us."[12]

7

Bartholomew: The Israelite without guile

THE name of St. Bartholomew is familiar, but chiefly because of the massacre by the French government of tens of thousands of French Protestants, or Huguenots, by which the apostle's feast day was disgraced in 1572. Familiar too is a grisly detail in *The Last Judgment* of Michelangelo, in which Bartholomew, bald, massive and grizzled, with an expression of outrage and indignation, gazes towards his Master as if angrily awaiting the discomfiture of his enemies. In his right hand the apostle holds aloft the knife with which he was skinned alive, and in his left his empty, rumpled skin, the token of his martyrdom. Yet, if most people, familiar both with the painting and with the Huguenot holocaust, were asked who St. Bartholomew was, they would be mute.

It is only since the ninth century that the apostle whom John calls Nathanael has been identified with Bartholomew, who is identified as one of the Twelve by Matthew, Mark and Luke. It was an obscure writer by the name of Elias of Damascus who first made the link. Since the synoptic Gospels as well as Acts always mention Bartholomew along with Philip, and since, in John's Gospel, it is Philip who first introduces Nathanael to the

Savior, this hypothesis does not seem unreasonable to many scholars. The assumption is strengthened by the fact that Bartholomew is a patronymic, meaning "Son of Tolmai." Whether Bartholomew is identified with Nathanael or not, he had to have a first name, and Nathanael, which means "God has given" in Hebrew, is a first name. Thus, the man whose call to apostleship is described by John did not quickly die or fade into oblivion, but is likely the same man whom the other evangelists identify as Bartholomew.

If Nathanael is to be identified with Bartholomew, we can learn something of his character from the first chapter of John. Jesus had just been baptized by John the Baptist at Bethabara. Two days later, having called Andrew, Peter and Philip, Jesus decided to begin the trek of more than seventy miles from Bethabara in Judea to Cana in Galilee. When they reached Cana, Philip went to the home of his friend Nathanael and announced, "We have found the one Moses spoke of in the law — the prophets too — Jesus, son of Joseph, from Nazareth." (Jn. 1:45)

Nathanael was a pious Jew who lived in daily expectation of the coming of the Messiah. He was evidently a close friend of Philip, and a disciple of John the Baptist. It was likely that Nathanael, even though his home at Cana was twelve miles away from the Sea of Galilee and twenty miles from Philip's home in Bethsaida, knew Philip through the fishing business. They may have worked on the same vessel or perhaps they were employed either by Peter or Zebedee. Nathanael may have been inclined to identify John the Baptist with the man who was to restore Israel. This might explain his reaction when Philip told him that the Messiah was not John, but rather a rabbi from the neighboring village of Nazareth.

"Can anything good come from Nazareth?" was Nathanael's first response. It is not exactly clear what was going through Nathanael's mind when he said this.

Nazareth was about nine miles from Cana, and some scholars have thought that Nathanael might have at first resented the fact that the Messiah was from a neighboring village rather than his own. "Why do *they* deserve that honor? I've never known of anything good ever coming out of *that* place!" Perhaps Nathanael knew people at Nazareth whom he did not like or perhaps he had undergone some unpleasant experiences there.

Nathanael went at once with Philip to meet Jesus. "This man is a true Israelite," said Jesus. "There is no guile in him." (Jn. 1:47) "Israelite" was popularly interpreted in those days as "a man who sees God." It was also associated with the cunning Jacob, the Old Testament patriarch who was given the name Israel after a vision of God. Jesus was basically saying, "You are a true Israelite in that you are a man who sees God, but unlike the patriarch Israel, you are a man without guile." Nathanael was evidently a man well-known for impeccable honesty, as a man who never "put up a front" to his true feelings.

"How do you know me?" Nathanael asked. He had never met Jesus before and yet this rabbi had accurately read his character.

"Before Philip called you, I saw you under the fig tree."

This statement immediately elicited from Nathanael the response, "Rabbi, you are the Son of God. You are the King of Israel."

"Do you believe just because I told you I saw you under the fig tree? You shall see much greater things than that. I solemnly assure you, you shall see the sky opened and the angels of God ascending and descending on the Son of Man." (Jn. 1:48-51)

Jesus again was referring to Jacob. We will recall that Jacob was a cunning, devious "operator," who tricked his father into disinheriting his older brother in favor of himself. When the brother, Esau, found out, Jacob was forced to flee for his life. On a deserted road, he lay down to sleep with a stone beneath his head for a pillow. There he dreamt he saw a ladder which rested on the ground with its top reaching to heaven and on the ladder were angels going up and down. (Gen. 28:12) It was then that the Lord identified himself to Jacob and promised to bless him and his posterity.

When Jesus told Nathanael that he would see angels ascending and descending "upon the Son of Man," he was indicating to him that He was the ladder between heaven and earth and that Bartholomew would shortly share in this revelation. To see Jesus as the ladder to heaven would be a thing far greater than even Jacob experienced.

That meeting between Jesus and Nathanael at Cana was the only meaningful reference to Nathanael in Scripture. John briefly mentioned him again in the twenty-first chapter when he included him among the apostles who, early one morning after the Resurrection, were fishing in the Sea of Galilee when Jesus called them in the darkness from the beach and directed them to a miraculous catch of fish. Even though it was too dark to make out the form and features of the man on the beach, the apostles knew then that it was their Lord. Matthew, Mark and Luke simply stated that one of the apostles was named Bartholomew. They never quoted him or recounted any incident in which he was a participant.

There is little to be said about the background of the man whose full name was likely Nathanael bar Tolmai of Cana. From his patronymic, we can tell that his father was named Tolmai or Talmai. Because one of the many wives of King David was Maacah, daughter of King Talmai of Geshur, some commentators have tried to suggest that Bartholomew was a royal prince who worked in perfect harmony with simple fishermen. The connection with David cannot be proved, however, and even if he had been a descendant of David he would not likely have been of greater wealth or higher social standing than the other apostles. After all, Jesus, the humble carpenter, was a descendant of David, and so were Matthew, James the Less, John, James the Great and possibly Thomas. Bartholomew was almost certainly not a man of wealth, but, like his fellows, a fisherman.

Of Bartholomew's later career, both Jerome and Chrysostom wrote that the apostle preached for a time in Lycaonia, before moving on to Armenia. Lycaonia was a region in central Asia Minor (now a part of Turkey) which rested on a tall plateau. It was a poor and backward region, infested with bandits in the first century. From Acts we learn that Paul and Barnabas preached there and that the most important cities were Derbe, Lystra and Iconium. Their population included Jews as well as a native pagan element whose members spoke a dialect of their own. Paul and Barnabas were there between A.D. 46 and 48. Despite stiff opposition from many of the Jews, the two apostles made many converts and established congregations with elders (priests) in each of the cities. Bartholomew may have visited these cities at a later date, and established additional congregations and ordained more elders.

Not only Jerome and Chrysostom, but also Isidore of Seville and his contemporary, "Pseudo-Sophronius," held that Bartholomew ministered in Armenia, some 400 miles northeast of Lycaonia. As we will see in a following chapter, Christianity was introduced to Armenia early, possibly in the A.D. 40s. Several apostles evidently preached and taught at some time or other in this kingdom, the area of which is today divided among the nations of Turkey, Iran, Iraq and the Soviet Union. The tradition that Bartholomew actually died at Albanopolis (Derbend) in Armenia is probably untenable, since the king who martyred him has been shown convincingly by an Indian scholar to have reigned in India, not Armenia.

If Bartholomew assisted Philip in Hierapolis in Phrygia, it could have only been in A.D. 58 or 59, at the very beginning of Philip's ministry there. It would have meant that he traveled west from Armenia into Asia Minor. He cannot have stayed there very long, since it is quite likely that he reached India by A.D. 60.

Indeed, the firmest traditions about Bartholomew's field of activities placed him in India. Both Eusebius and Jerome spoke of a scholar by the name of Pantanaeus, who, at the request of a native community of Christians there, was sent to India by Demetrius, bishop of Alexandria, around A.D. 180. When Pantanaeus arrived, to his amazement he found a copy of the Gospel of Matthew, written in Hebrew, which had been brought there by the apostle Bartholomew.[1]

The Apostolic Acts of Abdias preserves a tradition about Bartholomew's work in India. It also gives us a rather detailed description of the apostle's appearance. Bartholomew is described as a man of medium height (which might have meant a few inches over five feet!), with a very fair complexion (at least, according to the Indians) and black curly hair contrasting with a big gray beard. His face was dominated by a long straight nose, and he had a powerful, trumpet-like voice. Bartholomew was evidently a man of ascetical habits. The natives alleged that he wore the same shoes and clothing for twenty-six years without a change and that he prayed 100 times a day and 100 times a night. Allowing for some exaggeration, this would confirm his identification with Nathanael, who had been a disciple of the ascetic and self-denying John the Baptist. Despite this severity of life, the *Acts of Abdias* affirms that Bartholomew was a friendly, cheerful man and also a skillful linguist who "knows all languages."[2]

According to this account, while in India Bartholomew encountered the unfortunate daughter of King Polymius, who was "a lunatic who bit everyone." Polymius, having heard of Bartholomew's reputation as a holy man, begged him to help his daughter. It seems as if the madwoman was kept in a cage, like an animal, and was so violent that everyone who knew her was fearful when the apostle insisted that she be released. When she was, Bartholomew healed her and won the right from Polymius to preach the Gospel freely in his territory.

The people in the realm of Polymius worshiped the goddess Astaroth. Barthlomew, as Elijah had done centuries before in a contest with the priests of Baal, assembled a large crowd before the image of the goddess. Then he commanded the deity to show itself. Almost at once the statue shattered spontaneously and an angel appeared to sign "the four corners of the temple with a cross." Then the angel revealed the exorcised demon-deity to the crowd. The fiend was totally black, "sharp-faced, with a long beard, hair to the feet, fiery eyes . . . *and* spiky wings." It was breathing fire and brimstone. The angel bound the demon with chains and "sent him away howling." When King Polymius saw this, he was converted along with hundreds of other onlookers and was baptized that same day by Bartholomew.

Bartholomew did not live to enjoy a long ministry in India. When Polymius' brother Astriagis, who seemed to be more powerful, got wind of the baptisms, he made war on the new Christian community. Bartholomew was beaten with clubs, skinned alive and finally beheaded.[3]

An Indian scholar by the name of A.C. Perumalil did extensive research on this legend, studying ancient coins and other archaelogical artifacts, and pronounced the story essentially true in a monograph published in the

1950s. Citing Sophronius, who stated that Bartholomew preached the Gospel "to those Indians who are called 'the Happy,' '' Perumalil located the site of the apostle's labors in a city-state known as Kalyana, but called by the Romans "India Felix" or "Happy India." A flourishing city-state on the west coast of India, near modern Bombay, it had commercial dealings with the Arabs as well as the huge Roman and Iranian Empires. Perumalil found evidence that in the sixth century there was a flourishing population of Christians there, with a bishop appointed from the patriarchate of Babylon.

Perumalil speculated that Bartholomew reached Kalyana by joining a group of traders sailing from one of the Persian gulf harbors. King Polymius was identified with Pulumayi, a historical figure who was governor of Kalyana until his death around A.D. 62. Kalyana was evidently a client state of the Satavahana dynasty of Paithan, which ruled the area around modern Bombay. The king was Aristakarman. Perumalil was convinced that Astriagis was a Latinization of the name of the Indian king. The name of the local goddess, Astaroth, was similar to that of a Middle Eastern fertility deity, Ashtoreth, mentioned in the Old Testament, but Perumalil thought, in the case of the *Acts of Abdias,* she was to be identified with Astamurti, a Hindu deity who was worshiped by most of the natives of Kalyana.[4] Thus, Perumalil was convinced that Bartholomew did reach India, that he ministered in Kalyana, converted the governor Pulumayi, but angered the king, Pulumayi's brother Aristakarman, who put the apostle to death.

Briefly tracing Bartholomew's possible career, we have no idea when he left Palestine. Probably by the A.D. 50s he was in Asia Minor, preaching in some of the Lycaonian churches founded by Paul. From there he moved east into Armenia, where Christianity was already flourishing and where other apostles were laboring. Then he journeyed west again to join briefly his old friend Philip, who had just come to preside over the churches of Phrygia. Then, around A.D. 59 or 60, he undertook the most rigorous journey of all. Perhaps he had heard of a colony of Jews in the area known as India Felix. Perhaps he had met someone in Hierapolis or Armenia who hailed from that area and begged him to bring the Good News to his family and friends. For whatever reason, Bartholomew traveled laboriously over land into the Iranian Empire to one of the ports on the Persian Gulf. From there he sailed to the port of Kalyana, bearing with him a copy, in Hebrew, of St. Matthew's Gospel. There he founded a Christian community. After but a year or two of ministry there, Bartholomew, who enjoyed the favor of the local governor, incurred the wrath of the king, who had the apostle skinned alive and crucified on August 24, A.D. 62, when Bartholomew was probably in his late fifties. The Christian community he founded remained at least five centuries, presided over by a bishop appointed by the patriarch of Babylon. Because of the horrible manner of his death, Bartholomew is usually shown in sacred art holding a knife in one hand and his skin draped over the other arm.

8

Thomas: Apostle to the Orient

ABOUT all that most people know about the apostle Thomas is that he was "The Doubter." "Doubting Thomas" is frequently imagined as a dour, pessimistic man, disinclined to believe, even in the face of overwhelming evidence, the man who tried to throw the monkey wrench into the engine of Easter joy. Actually, the information which the New Testament provides about Thomas does not lead the reader to such a conclusion. Like most of the Twelve, Thomas was simply mentioned a few times, but those incidents present a picture of a clearheaded man of courage and intellect.

We know more about the life of Thomas after Calvary than we do about any other apostle except for Peter and John. The interesting fact about Thomas is that almost all of his ministry took place outside the Roman Empire and nearly all our sources about him are non-Western. Before we concern ourselves with Thomas' ministry in Osroene, Armenia, Iran, India and Southeast Asia, let us examine what there is to learn about him from New Testament sources.

Thomas was merely mentioned as one of the Twelve by Matthew, Mark and Luke. John related four incidents in which Thomas was involved, some of which give small clues to his character. The first was associated with the raising of Lazarus. During the winter of A.D. 31-32, Jesus

119

was run out of Jerusalem after teaching that "the Father and I are one." (Jn. 10:30) Jesus knew, and all His disciples knew, that the next time He set foot in Jerusalem He would be killed. A few months later, however, Jesus received word that His great friend Lazarus was critically ill. Lazarus and his family lived in Bethany, a suburb two miles outside Jerusalem, which was a four-day journey from the place where Jesus was ministering at the time. Although the message stated that Lazarus was very ill, Jesus told the Twelve that their friend was then in fact dead. Nevertheless, the Lord announced His intention of going to Bethany. Most of the Twelve were alarmed that their Master was going to risk their lives by going into hostile territory, especially when it was too late to help Lazarus. It was only Thomas who showed no reluctance to go. It was he who rallied the other apostles, affirming, "Let us go along, to die with him." (Jn. 11:16)

"Thomas was an awfully pessimistic man," someone might say. This was not necessarily the case. Thomas' pessimism was born of prudence and common sense. All the apostles knew that Jesus was a dead man if He set foot in Jerusalem — or *near* Jerusalem again. They knew that there was a real possibility that they would be killed with Him. Thomas was not the only apostle who sensed that his life would be endangered if he went with Jesus to Bethany; on the contrary, he was the only one of the Twelve who, despite a clear and present danger, was willing to put his life on the line for his Master. This incident revealed Thomas not as a man of doubt and distrust, but of prudence, courage and loyalty.

The second mention of Thomas by John was set in Jerusalem just before the Passion. Jesus had gone to Bethany and raised up Lazarus; then, amidst stupendous demonstrations of acclaim following the miracle, He entered Jerusalem for the Passover. After the Last Supper,

Jesus declared, "Do not let your hearts be troubled. Have faith in God and faith in me. In my Father's house there are many dwelling places; otherwise, how could I have told you that I was going to prepare a place for you? I am indeed going to prepare a place for you, and then I shall come back to take you with me, that where I am you also may be. You know the road that leads where I go." (Jn. 14:1-4)

Thomas did not know what Jesus was talking about and asked, "Lord, we do not know where you are going. How can we know the way?" (Jn. 14:5) This prompted Jesus to declare, "I am the way, and the truth, and the life; no one comes to the Father but through me." (Jn. 14:6)

The most famous incident involving Thomas earned him the reputation of "The Doubter." The Lord had appeared after His Resurrection to all the apostles except Thomas, who was absent at the time when his ten colleagues were together. When told of the appearance of the Risen Lord, Thomas replied, "I will never believe it without probing the nailprints in his hands, without putting my finger in the nailmarks and my hand into his side." (Jn. 20:25)

Thomas' reaction was eminently reasonable. He knew as well as anybody else that people who were really and truly dead did not come to life again. Thomas had seen the tortured cadaver of his Master with its wounds in the hands, feet and side. He had no doubts at all that Jesus was dead. As to His alleged Resurrection, what was he to believe? Perhaps his colleagues had seen a ghost. Perhaps they were telling him of a purely intellectual or spiritual experience. Perhaps someone was playing tricks on them. Perhaps they were, for some reason, trying to make a fool of him. The proof that Thomas demanded was quite reasonable. He wanted to have the same experience that his colleagues had in order to prove to himself that the Resurrection was physical and material, rather than intellectual. When Jesus did appear to him and Thomas was convinced that he was seeing alive the same body that had died under torture on the cross, he was persuaded and declared, "My Lord and my God!"

Thomas' reaction was that of a sensible man. It is true that Jesus told him, "Blest are they who have not seen and have believed." (Jn. 20:29) The Lord was referring here to posterity, to those whom the Twelve would evangelize. Jesus does not have to make a special Resurrection appearance to each human being. The testimony of the Twelve, and other apostles, such as Paul and James the Righteous, is sufficient for subsequent generations. The Resurrection is experienced and questioned by men and women who are at first confused and incredulous. There is as much evidence for the Resurrection as there is for any other event of that time, such as the assassination of Caesar or the suicide of Cleopatra. The incident involving Thomas' "doubting" shows him a practical man of common sense who demanded empirical proof.

St. Thomas was mentioned a final time, in the twenty-first chapter of John, where he was included in the fishing expedition of the Sea of Galilee to which Jesus appeared after His Resurrection. He was simply named, and we learn nothing of his personality from this incident.

The only other information we have about Thomas from the New Testament is that he was called "Didymus," or "The Twin." Actually, this is simply a translation into Greek of the Hebrew name "Thomas," which also means "twin." This was obviously not a given name, but a surname, like "Peter" and "Boanerges." We learn from Eusebius as well as from early Syrian writings that Thomas' given name was Judah, or Jude.

We do not know where Thomas was born. *The Acts of*

Thomas, written about A.D. 200, describes Thomas as a carpenter and a member of Jesus' immediate family. All the other apostles we have discussed so far, except possibly James the Less, were fishermen.

Thomas had one of the most active ministries of any of the Twelve. Eusebius wrote that almost immediately after Pentecost, Thomas was instrumental in evangelizing the nation of Osroene, which lay to the north of Palestine, in what is now eastern Turkey, between the Roman and Iranian Empires. Eusebius cited documents which still existed in his day in the Archive of Edessa, the capital of Osroene, which described the conversion of Prince Abgar the Black, who ruled there between A.D. 13 and 50. Among those papers was a transcript of a letter which Abgar had written to Jesus. Abgar was ill with a distemper, impervious to the art of all the physicians of his day, and wrote to Jesus that he had heard "about the cures you perform without drugs and herbs." He continued:

> If the report is true, you make the blind see again and the lame walk about; you cleanse lepers, expel unclean spirits and demons, cure those suffering from chronic and painful diseases, and raise the dead. When I heard all this about you, I concluded that one of two things must be true — either you are God and come down from heaven to do these things, or you are God's Son doing them. Accordingly I am writing to beg you to come to me, whatever the inconvenience, and cure the disorder from which I suffer. I may add that I understand the Jews are treating you with contempt and desire to injure you. My city is very small, but highly esteemed, adequate for us both.[1]

According to the papers on file in the Edessan Archive, Jesus had sent Abgar the following reply, orally, through the messenger who had dispatched the letter from the prince: "Happy are you who believed in me without having seen me! For it is written of me that those who have seen me will not believe in me, and that those who have not seen will believe and live. As to your request that I should come to you, I must complete all that I was sent to do here, and, on completing it, must at once be taken up to the One who sent me. When I have been taken up I will send you one of my disciples to cure your disorder and bring life to you and those with you."[2]

Eusebius recounted that it was Thomas who urged his colleague Jude Thaddaeus to go to Edessa to heal the king and preach to the people. Many believed, as we shall discuss in the chapter on Thaddaeus, that the records that Eusebius saw in the Edessan Archive were forgeries perpetrated to invent an "apostolic succession" for a church that later separated from Rome. However, there are very ancient traditions that not only Thaddaeus but also Thomas ministered in Osroene and the neighboring kingdom of Armenia. It is a fact that the Church of the East and Assyria has traced the succession of its bishops back to Thomas. Their first two bishops, Abris and James I, were first cousins of Jesus.

Thomas evidently left Jerusalem early and spent many years ministering in Osroene, whose inhabitants spoke Syriac (a tongue closely related to Aramaic) and where there were many Jews. He also made trips into the adjoining kingdom of Armenia. Thomas may have returned to Jerusalem briefly in the late A.D. 40s, before moving on to India.

The earliest source for knowledge of Thomas' ministry in India is a Syriac document, probably written in Edessa around A.D. 200, known as *The Acts of Thomas*. Described as a historical novel, a piece of fiction written for entertainment, it is based on historical fact. Thomas was a national hero for the Christians of Osroene and they enjoyed reading about the founder of their national Church. In addition to *The Acts of Thomas,* a document attributed to the third-century author Hippolytus also located Thomas' ministry in India as well as Iran,[3] and Eusebius, who wrote a century later, stated that Thomas was sent to Parthia (Iran) but does not mention India.[4]

When merchants and missionaries from Portugal arrived in India in the sixteenth century, they were astonished to find a flourishing community of Christians who steadfastly maintained that their Church, the Church of Malabar, had been founded in the first century by St. Thomas. In 1533, the King of Portugal directed all of his missionaries to take down the local history of the Christians. It was soon discovered that there was a susbstantial body of tradition about Thomas in India. There were some ancient books, written in Syriac, as well as songs and a huge corpus of oral tradition. Interviews were conducted with the bishop of the Church of Malabar, the *Abuna,* whose title meant "Our Father." He stated that Thomas was sent by Christ to India, that he had set out from Jerusalem in the company of Bartholomew and Jude Thaddaeus. While Thaddaeus and Bartholomew remained in the Middle East, Thomas arrived at the western coast of India, then went to China, where he founded a church in Peking. On returning to India, he converted "thousands and thousands" on the eastern coast before he was martyred.[5]

Some scholars scoff at these traditions. Christianity in India, they say, dates only from the fourth century, when missionaries arrived from Syria. It is their belief that since the Church in Edessa was almost certainly founded by Thomas, and traces its apostolic successors to him, the ignorant Indians gradually convinced themselves that the apostle had actually visited their land. Even the most cautious historian, however, will have to concede that the chances that Thomas was active in India are at least fifty-fifty. The dispassionate Bishop Leslie W. Brown declared in 1956:

> The tradition of St. Thomas' death in South India is not entirely disproved, and no other place in the world claims the event. We cannot prove that the Apostle worked in South India any more than we can disprove the fact; but the presence of Christians of undoubtedly ancient origin holding firmly to the tradition, the proof of very considerable commercial contact between the western world and the Malabar coast in the first century of our era, and the probable presence of Jewish colonies at the same time, may for some incline the balance to the belief that the truth of the tradition is a reasonable probability.[6]

Since Bishop Brown wrote, archaeological finds have indicated that Christianity in India certainly predated the fourth century. It has been discovered that Pallivaanavar, a king of southwestern India in the middle of the second century, was a Christian.[7]

Moreover, an ancient Syriac document, dating from the third century and called *The Doctrines of the Apostles,* recounted that "India and all its own countries and those bordering even to the farthest sea, received the Apostles' hand of priesthood from Judas Thomas, who was Guide and Ruler in the Church which he built there and ministered there."[8] A scholar named A. Mingana, writing in 1926, declared, "It is the constant tradition of the Eastern Church that the Apostle Thomas evangelized India, and there is no historian, no poet, no breviary, no liturgy, and no writer of any kind, who, having the opportunity of speaking of Thomas, does not associate his name with India."[9]

The Acts of Thomas revolved around the apostle's

ministry in northwestern India — in what is now called the Punjab — at the court of King Gundaphorus. For years no one believed that such a king ever lived, until, in the nineteenth century, coins dating to the first century were found in northern India bearing his name in Greek characters. We now know that Gundaphorus (or Gudnaphar) was an Iranian prince who ruled in the middle of the first century in what is now Pakistan and northwestern India. The Iranian Empire was then a loose confederation of principalities and the realm of Gundaphorus marked the southeastern extent. The Iranian (or Persian) Empire was generally called Parthia by the Romans, and this would explain Eusebius' identification of Thomas' field of activity as Parthia rather than India.

In reconstructing Thomas' activities in north India, we will assume that *The Acts of Thomas* is relatively accurate in its essentials. Two scholars named Farquhar and Garitte wrote an interesting study in 1972 relating *The Acts of Thomas* to known historical facts.

Thomas evidently returned from Osroene to Jerusalem in A.D. 49, perhaps for the Council of Jerusalem. While in Jerusalem, he met a Jewish Christian named Abban or Habban, whom Farquhar and Garitte identified as Gundaphorus' royal trade commissioner. Abban had been trying to spread the Gospel among the Hindus and Zoroastrians as well as the Jews of Taxila, the capital city of Gundaphorus' realms. Abban encouraged Thomas to return with him to India. Gundaphorus was looking for a master carpenter to construct a royal palace, and Thomas was known as a master carpenter who specialized in making ploughs, yokes, balances, pulleys, ships, oars, masts, as well as houses.

According to the *Acts of Thomas,* the apostle was unwilling at first to go, even when Christ appeared to him in a vision. Thomas asked: "How can I, a Jew, go and preach the Truth to Indians?" Christ answered: "Fear not, Thomas. Go to India and preach the word there, for my grace is with you," said Christ.[10]

Farquhar and Garitte felt that the account in the apocryphal *Acts* about Thomas being captured by Abban as a slave when he disobeyed the vision was fabrication. They also believed that Thomas and Abban sailed to Alexandria, an Egyptian port from which 120 ships sailed to India each year. In the spring of A.D. 49, the two men boarded a ship there and sailed up the Nile. After one day they arrived at the port of Andropolis. Eleven days after that they reached the port of Koptos, where they disembarked and traveled for a week in a caravan over desert terrain to the port of Myos-Hormos on the Red Sea. They left Myos-Hormos by ship in May and stopped at Okelis, on the east coast of the Red Sea, in early June. A few days later the ship reached the Gulf of Aden, where it picked up the full force of the monsoon winds blowing from the southwest. According to Farquhar and Garitte, "They would then have to endure more than a month of the worst sailing in the world, driven furiously over the tempestuous Arabian Sea by the irresistible monsoon, lashed by wild rainstorms, the heat and damp unendurable, many of the passengers sick and ill day and night."[11]

In mid-July, Thomas and Abban disembarked at Pattala, in northern India. Boarding a smaller boat, they sailed 1,300 miles north up the Indus River to Attock. From there they journeyed forty miles to the southeast on foot until in the late summer, after a trek of about five months, they arrived in Taxila. Known as "The Athens of India," Taxila was far to the north of Kalyana, where Bartholomew would later minister. Taxila traded with China as well as the Roman Empire. Greek was spoken there, as well as Indian and Iranian tongues. It was the home of a university where a number of eminent Hindu and Buddhist scholars taught.[12] Farquhar and Garitte were convinced that Thomas studied there and mastered the Punjabi language. "As soon as he was able to use the vernacular, he would meet groups of keenly interested educated men, from whose questions and answers he would learn a very great deal about the religious life of India; and day by day he would come to see more clearly how the grace of God had better be commended to the Hindu conscience and heart."[13]

Meanwhile, Thomas was engaged by Gundaphorus as a builder and architect. According to the *Acts of Thomas*, he was commissioned to build a palace and was given substantial appropriations. Thomas, instead of working on the building, traveled about the area, giving money to the poor, healing the sick, and teaching the "New God." When Gundaphorus heard about this, he summoned Thomas. "Have you finished my mansion yet?" he asked. Thomas replied in the affirmative. "Well," said the king, "when can we go and see it?" Thomas replied rather flippantly, "You cannot see it now, but when you depart this life you shall see it."

Thomas was about to be tortured to death by an enraged king when he was saved by an out-of-the-body experience of the king's brother Gad, who was suddenly taken ill and pronounced dead. When revived, however, Gad told his brother that he had seen the heavenly palace that Thomas had built for him. When he heard this, Gundaphorus believed and, along with his brother, was baptized.[14]

Thomas could have remained at Taxila for only a year or two, for it was in the early A.D. 50s that Gundaphorus was overthrown by the Kushans, who swept down out of China. The South Indians believed that Thomas arrived in their land in A.D. 52, so it is reasonable to assume that the apostle left Taxila when the Kushan menace became apparent. Farquhar and Garitte also believed that Abban and Gundaphorus gave Thomas letters of recommendation to the rulers of several South Indian principalities.

We must remember that India was not a united country in the first century. The subcontinent contained a number of independent kingdoms and principalities. The kingdoms of South India maintained close commercial contact with Rome in the first century. Large quantities of Roman pottery, beads, lamps, glass and coins have been uncovered by archaeologists at various sites there. They have found evidence that the princes of South India exported pepper, pearls, ivory, silk, spices and textiles to Rome in return for glass, tin, lead, wine and gold. There were three major kingdoms in South India in the first century: Pandyas, Keras (or Kerala) and Colas (or Chola). They were agrarian societies, almost constantly at war. Most people lived in small villages headed by a *sabha,* or council, which conducted local affairs. The cities were more cosmopolitan. In such urban centers as Cranganore and Nelcynda there were Greeks, Romans, Egyptians, Arabs and Jews, as well as Hindus. When Thomas arrived by ship at Cranganore, he undoubtedly followed the apostolic practice of seeking out members of the Jewish community.

The inhabitants of the Malabar Coast of India (the west coast) have many traditions about Thomas. One tradition is interesting to compare with an incident from the Syriac *Acts of Thomas.* According to the Middle Eastern document, Thomas, while still at the court of Gundaphorus, was attending a banquet when he was punched in the face by a cupbearer. Thomas told the offender, "My God will forgive you this injury in the world to come, but in this world He will show forth His wonders, and I shall even now see that hand which smote me dragged by dogs." Shortly afterward the cupbearer went outside to draw water and was attacked by a lion, which killed him and mauled his body. A big black dog gnawed on the mangled remains and walked into the banquet hall with the cup-bearer's right hand in his mouth.[15]

According to the South Indian version of the story, the apostle was present at the wedding feast of a local prince. In this version it was one of the king's ministers who slapped Thomas in the face when he saw the apostle in ec-stasy. Thomas then announced a "temporal punishment so that you can avoid an eternal one." The man went outside to wash his hands and was attacked by a tiger. The minis-ter was not killed, but his hand was bitten off. The man staggered, bleeding, into the banquet hall, followed by a dog carrying the severed member. According to this ver-sion, Thomas took the hand and miraculously reattached it.[16]

It is interesting to compare the versions. The second version was told to Portuguese missionaries as oral his-tory. The first was written down in Syriac in the third cen-tury. Are these stories different versions of the same event which arose independently of each other? Or did Syrian missionaries, familiar with the *Acts of Thomas,* translate the story into the native Tamil language, making certain adaptations to local culture?

The Indians of Malabar in the sixteenth century savored another gruesome legend about the apostle. The story goes that a Hindu kicked Thomas, and, as a penance, the apostle put a curse on him so that all his descendants "carried their legs swollen, full of . . . knots and loathsome corrugations, filled with pus."[17] And so the natives blamed the widespread incidence of elephantiasis on St. Thomas!

Another story, which reveals the apostle in a some-what less vindictive light, has to do with the resurrection of a dead boy. A Brahman priest, to spite Thomas, killed his own son and accused Thomas of putting a spell on the boy and thus ending his life. Thomas brought the boy to life again. After the child testified that it was his father and not the "holy man" who had done him in, the apostle asked the boy if he would rather live in this world or that from which he had just been summoned. When the boy replied, "The other," Thomas baptized him and the child died.[18]

The *Rabban Song,* which has been passed down orally by generations of Indian Christians, recounts Thomas' career in India in some detail. It states that the apostle arrived in India in late A.D. 49, stayed briefly, then went on to China. This generally agrees with several other Indian traditions. Such a trip would have occurred shortly after Thomas' arrival in South India. Farquhar and Garitte believe that it is unlikely that Thomas actually went to China proper — certainly not Peking — within the short space of perhaps a year allotted by the Indian narratives. They believe that he did evangelize in what are now Burma and Malaysia for a short time before returning to South India.

According to the *Rabban Song,* between A.D. 52 and 59 Thomas founded seven churches and baptized one king, forty Jews and some 3,000 Hindus. In the fall of A.D. 59 he went from the west to the east coast of India, where he settled for a time at Mylapore, and where he baptized King Choran of Lola and 700 other persons.

Early in A.D. 62, Thomas started a long series of missionary tours, similar to those that Paul had conducted in the Near East a few years earlier. He founded Christian colonies in the cities of Cranganore, Kottakayal, Kokomangalam, Kollom, Niranam, and Chayal. Like Paul, Thomas also had his greatest success in cities and towns. Between A.D. 62 and 69, Thomas and his disciples are reputed to have baptized more than 17,000 Hindus. The *Rabban Song* also catalogues the miracles worked by Thomas during this period: nineteen dead persons raised,

260 successful exorcisms, 230 lepers healed, 250 blind restored to sight, 220 paralytics cured and 250 other persons ill with various incurable maladies healed. Thomas ordained priests and bishops, including Kepa, who came from the royal family of Kerala and came to be bishop of Cranganore.[19]

In A.D. 69, Thomas settled permanently in Mylapore. He was by then at least in his sixties and getting too old for extensive travel under rugged and primitive conditions. Allowing for some exaggeration in the *Rabban Song* and other sources, the apostle conducted a ministry similar to Paul's, with extensive travel and many miraculous occurrences. Even the Hindus considered him a "holy man." Indeed, according to *The Acts of Thomas,* the apostle was very much like Bartholomew and James the Righteous, given to fasting and long periods of prayer. He is said to have eaten only bread and water and never to have owned more than one garment at one time. This leads one to speculate that he too had once been a disciple of the Baptist. According to the traditions of the "St. Thomas Christians" of Malabar, Thomas forbade any sort of pictures or images, but decorated his houses of worship with the symbol of the cross. This is interesting in light of the fact that the cross did not emerge as a religious symbol in the Roman Empire until the fourth century, after the Emperor Constantine abolished it as a means of execution.

According to most Indian traditions, Thomas died of stab wounds on July 3, A.D. 72. The Brahman priests of Mylapore feared that Christianity would eclipse Hinduism. Several of their number found Thomas praying in a cave near his home and wounded him with a spear. The apostle dragged himself out of the cave, struggled some distance to a nearby chapel and, in the presence of several of his disciples, grasped a stone cross. According to an account noted by Marco Polo, Thomas prayed, "Lord, I thank Thee for all Thy mercies. Into Thy hands I commend my spirit," and entered into rest.[20] So closed the remarkable career of a remarkable man, a man who should be remembered not for being a "doubter," but for his faith and zeal.

9

Matthew:
The phantom apostle

ST. Matthew's name, among those of the Twelve, is one of the most familiar. This is doubtless because of his Gospel, which is generally considered to be the most popular and widely read of the four. Matthew, however, is among the apostles about whom we know the least, and even his beloved Gospel, as we know it today, is likely much altered from the form in which he originally penned it. For this reason we could refer to Matthew as "the phantom apostle," since behind the familiarity of his name there remains so little knowledge about his life and work.

The first three Gospels all give a brief account of Matthew's call. In Matthew's own Gospel we read how "Jesus saw a man named Matthew at the post where taxes were collected. He said to him, 'Follow me.' Matthew got up and followed him." (Mt. 9:9) Mark and Luke recount the same story, but identify the tax collector as Levi. All three accounts obviously refer to the same incident and the same man. Also, none of the lists of the apostles provided in the first three Gospels include the name of Levi. Therefore, the man in question, like most of his colleagues, was known by at least two names: Matthew and Levi. Levi is a common Jewish name, after the founder of one of the Twelve Tribes of Israel. Matthew is Greek for "gift of God." It is quite conceivable that a Jewish employee of the Roman government would go by a Greek name at work, and continue to use such a name when, later in life, he was involved in evangelical work among people of different races and cultures.

St. Mark tells us that Levi was a son of Alphaeus. This would make him a brother of James the Less and Simeon, and also a relative by marriage of Jesus. Whether Matthew was a native of Capernaum, where he was working at the time of his call, cannot be confirmed. Because of the family connection, it is unlikely that Matthew's call came like a bolt out of the blue. Most likely he was, like many of the apostles, well known to Jesus and his call came after earlier inquiries and conversations.

Matthew was, of course, a tax collector, an occupation greatly despised by his fellow Jews. After his call, when Matthew gave a big dinner for Jesus, the leaders of the Jewish community at Capernaum drew a reprimand from the Lord for complaining that He ate with "tax collectors and sinners." "The healthy do not need a doctor; sick people do. I have not come to invite the self-righteous to a change of heart, but sinners." (Lk. 5:31-32)

Roman taxation was handled by wealthy businessmen who paid a set fee for a contract to collect taxes in a specific jurisdiction. The tax contractor, or publican, was assigned a certain amount of money to collect within a given time. If he failed to raise the sum that his jurisdiction was assessed, he had to pay the deficit out of his pocket. Any excess, however, he was allowed to keep. Thus the Roman system of taxation lent itself to grave abuse. In order to make a profit (remember, he had already paid a sum for the privilege of collecting taxes) the publican had to demand more revenue than the government actually required. Ordinary people knew this and resented anyone connected with the internal revenue service of the day.

Matthew was not one of the "fat cats" who had bought a government contract, but was an employee of such an official. To use modern terminology, the publican would have been the commissioner of revenue for a certain section of the Roman Empire. Within that territory there would be divisions, or branch offices. Matthew was employed in the branch office at Capernaum, which was an important port on the Sea of Galilee. Such an office handled import and export duties, taxes on all goods bought and sold, taxes on all travelers entering or leaving town, road tolls, bridge tolls, harbor tolls, taxes on goods brought to market, and trade and professional licenses. The bureau of taxation in Capernaum probably employed a number of people. Exactly what Matthew's responsibilities were, Scripture does not say. He was able to give Jesus a lavish feast and he was sufficiently well-known among the townspeople. The fact that Jesus' appearance at his home drew a protest from community leaders leads to speculation that Matthew might have been the local bureau chief.

Matthew was thus despised by many patriotic Jews simply because of his position. He probably had nothing to do with setting the amount of assessment. Still, the fact that he worked for the corrupt Roman internal revenue service would, of course, have made him guilty in the eyes of the public, even if his personal conduct was above reproach (which it may or may not have been). Moreover, the very fact that he worked for the Romans made him a traitor in the eyes of many a Palestinian patriot. Thus Jesus' call of a man alleged to have grown prosperous by cheating his own people did not serve to ingratiate the Lord to many leaders of the Jewish community.

Of Matthew's subsequent career, either during the earthly ministry of Jesus or after His Resurrection, we know little except for the fact that he wrote a Gospel. That he did is almost the universal testimony of the early Christian Fathers. Papias, who wrote in the early second century, was quoted by Eusebius as saying, "Matthew compiled *The Sayings* in the Aramaic language, and everyone translated them as well as he could."[1] Irenaeus maintained that Matthew published a written Gospel for the Hebrews in their own tongue, while Peter and Paul were preaching the Gospel in Rome and founding the Church there.[2] Tertullian and Origen also affirmed that Matthew wrote a Gospel. Eusebius, as we saw in the chapter on Bartholomew, mentioned Pantanaeus, a missionary to India, who found a copy of Matthew's Gospel there around A.D. 180. Jerome wrote perhaps the most extensive account of the origin of Matthew's Gospel. Writing in A.D. 392 he declared:

> Matthew, also called Levi, Apostle and aforetimes publican, composed a gospel of Christ at first published in Judaea in Hebrew for the sake of those of the circumcision who believed, but this was afterwards translated into Greek, though by what author is uncertain. The Hebrew itself has been preserved until the present day in the library at Caesarea which Pamphilius so diligently gathered. I have also had the opportunity of having the volume described to me by the Nazarenes of Beroea, a city of Syria, who use it. In this it is to be noted that wherever the Evangelist, whether on his own account or in the person of our Lord the Savior, quotes the testimony of the Old Testament, he does not follow the authority of the translators of the Septuagint, but the Hebrew.[3]

So it seems undeniable that Matthew wrote a Gospel for Jewish Christians, probably between A.D. 50 and 70, in or near Jerusalem, and in the Aramaic tongue which, although almost extinct today, was the everyday language of Jews in Palestine and Syria in the first century. Also, this Gospel was reworked by someone other than Matthew into a Greek version, which is the form in which we know the Gospel today. The Aramaic version from Matthew's pen, which still existed in the fifth century, has long since vanished.

The most quoted of all the Gospels, the Gospel according to St. Matthew emphasized the fulfillment of Old Testament prophecy. The formula, "That the word might be fulfilled which was spoken by the Lord through the prophet," was used thirteen times by Matthew. As the commentator Floyd V. Filson declared, "Matthew links the New Testament with the Old Testament and at the same time insists that God's central act in Jesus Christ brings the new age."[4] In addition, Filson points out, "The atmosphere of this Gospel is such as to have a special point for those who had come from Judaism and needed assurance that the Christian gospel not only fulfilled the Old Testament promises, but also gave the full statement of the will of God on points where the Old Testament Law was inadequate."[5]

Because the Gospel does not translate easily into Aramaic and because approximately half of the forty-odd Old Testament quotations are (contrary to what Jerome says about the original) from the Greek translation known as the Septuagint, some scholars have expressed doubt as to whether Matthew's Gospel, as we know it today, is a direct translation from the original. Some feel that there is good reason to believe that our present Gospel was compiled late in the first century by an editor who drew upon Matthew's work as well as upon St. Mark's. This question is, of course, almost incapable of satisfactory resolution. It does seem certain, however, that Matthew did compile a collection of the sayings of Christ in the Aramaic tongue, and that this work was later incorporated into the Greek composition which we know today as St. Matthew's Gospel.

We know almost nothing about Matthew as a person or about his career after Calvary. He was probably the only one of the Twelve Apostles for whose later life there emerged no coherent tradition. Clement of Alexandria was the only Church Father who had anything to say about Matthew's personality. Like James the Righteous, Thomas and Bartholomew, Matthew was a man of austere personal habits, a vegetarian who lived on nuts, seeds and vegetables. As for his field of activity, Clement said that Matthew ministered to the Jewish Christian community in Palestine for fifteen years. Irenaeus and Jerome also affirmed that Matthew ministered to Jewish converts.

Various traditions placed Matthew's evangelical labors in such diverse places as Iran, Macedonia, Egypt, Syria and Ethiopia. Most of them affirmed that he died a martyr's death under Domitian, but some said this took place in Ethiopia, others in Iran, still others in the Roman Empire. Clement of Alexandria maintained that Matthew died a natural death in extreme old age.

It is reasonable to assume that Matthew ministered to the Jewish Christian community for a number of years. If we take the figure of fifteen given us by Clement, this takes us to A.D. 47. Matthew certainly does not seem to have been a prominent figure in Jerusalem during the time that Paul refers to James the Righteous, Peter and John as the "pillars" of the Church there, nor is he mentioned in Acts, except in the list of the apostles. Perhaps Matthew traveled extensively to Jewish colonies throughout the Near East. Since it seems that he seldom if ever crossed paths with Paul (who never mentions him), it is possible that Matthew visited Jewish colonies in other regions, such as Egypt. While there, it is possible that he met and converted Jews from Ethiopia and that they invited him to take his ministry to their homeland.

In the first century, Ethiopia was a flourishing independent kingdom, usually known as Axum, after its capital city. It included not only the territory of modern Ethiopia and Somalia, but also what is now southwestern Saudi Arabia. Axum had trade dealings with the Roman Empire and a major port, Adulis, on the Red Sea. Most important, as we have seen in the conversion of the finance minister by Philip, there was a large population of Jews there, and this makes it not unlikely that at least one of the apostles would have tried to work with the Ethiopian Jews.

There are two substantial fanciful accounts of Matthew in Ethiopia. One of them comes from *The Apostolic History of Abdias*. Matthew had came to a city called Naddaver, apparently at the invitation of the finance minister who had been converted by Philip. In this account, he is called Candacis, which is simply Latin for "belonging to Candace," or the queen. The queen is not mentioned in the *History of Abdias,* which speaks of a pagan king, Aeglippus, who was dominated by two "magicians," Zaroes and Arfaxat; these magicians reportedly were able to strike their adversaries with paralysis, blindness and deafness, and also charmed snakes. Matthew, who had the gift of tongues, was able to preach to the people in their native dialect almost immediately and soon incurred the hostility of the two medicine men. They approached Matthew with two huge snakes, which promptly fell motionless at the apostle's feet. Matthew challenged Zaroes and Arfaxat to rouse the snakes, but they could not.[6]

Later Matthew raised the son of King Aeglippus from the dead. When the people tried to sacrifice to the apostle as a god, Matthew dissuaded them and urged them to build a church, which he named the Church of the Resurrection. Matthew stayed in Ethiopia twenty-three years, where he ordained clergy, founded churches and baptized the entire royal family. The people totally rejected their tribal religion, thus forcing Zaroes and Arfaxat to flee to Iran.

According to the *History of Abdias,* Matthew was martyred under Aeglippus' brother and successor, Hyrtaeus. Hyrtaeus wanted to marry his own niece, Aeglippus' daughter Ephigenia, who had become a nun and was presiding over a convent of two hundred "sacred virgins." Hyrtaeus offered Matthew half his kingdom to persuade Ephigenia to marry him. When Matthew refused to cooperate, Hyrtaeus ordered one of his soldiers to stab Matthew in the back, killing him.[7]

The sixth-century *Martyrdom of Matthew* gives a slightly different version. It recounts the apostle's martyrdom at the hands of a tribe of cannibals. Ordered by Jesus to the "city of man-eaters," Matthew was met at the "gate of the city" by the wife, son and daughter-in-law of the chief, all of whom were possessed by devils. "The devils cried out and threatened Matthew," but the apostle exorcised all three. Somehow, among these cannibals there lived a Christian bishop named Plato, who came out to meet Matthew "with all the clergy." Matthew then preached to the cannibals and converted and baptized them.

The chief, who bore the Greco-Latin name of Phulbanus, was enraged, however, and decided to burn Matthew alive. He seized the apostle and crucified him, nailing him to the ground, pouring flammable substances on him and setting him ablaze. The fire flared up, took the form of a snake and chased the chief all the way up to his palace, where he cried to Matthew for help. The apostle, still alive, "rebuked the fire," and died. The fire was extinguished and Matthew's body — even his clothing — was found intact, and the chief had the remains brought into his palace. Then, "when they reached the palace, Matthew was seen to rise from the bier and ascend to heaven, led by a beautiful child and twelve men in crowns."[8]

It is obvious that the author of the *Martyrdom of*

Matthew was writing pure fiction for entertainment's sake, and that even the *History of Abdias* is more fancy than fact. It is, however, conceivable that Matthew lived among the Jews of Ethiopia for twenty-three years, albeit somewhat less dramatically. If he established a hierarchy, there was no record made of its lasting, since Ethiopia did not become officially a Christian nation until the time of King Ezana in the fourth century.

Matthew probably did not die in Ethiopia. Toward the end of his life he may have gone to Iran (also known as Parthia and Persia). Hippolytus stated that Matthew died, apparently a natural death, in Hierees in Persia.[9] Taking into account Clement's contention that Matthew died naturally at a great age, and other traditions that he died during the time of Domitian (who had, of course, no jurisdiction over Iran), there is a good case for believing that Matthew's death around A.D. 90 was not a martyrdom.

Matthew's history, however, is a shadowy one. If his Gospel is any clue to his character, he seems to have ministered primarily to Jews, but if the lack of reference to him by Paul has any significance, it appears as if Matthew's sphere of activity was not in the Mediterranean. For lack of any other evidence, we can speculate that he went, over a period of many years, from Egypt to Ethiopia and then to Iran, where he died. Still, the facts remain so vague and shaky that Matthew remains to us a "phantom apostle."

10

Simon and Jude: Martyrs in Iran

THE only two apostles to die together were St. Simon and St. Jude. For this reason, they are commemorated on a joint feast day in the Roman Catholic, Anglican and Lutheran denominations of Christendom. As is the case with most of the apostles, what we know about them comes from diverse strains of tradition recorded many years after their passing.

Matthew referred to St. Simon as *Kananaios,* as did St. Mark. St. Luke, however, both in his Gospel and in Acts, called him "The Zealot." Some interpreted the Greek word *Kananaios* to indicate that Simon was, like Nathanael Bartholomew, a native of the town of Cana. *Kananaios* is actually a transliteration of the Aramaic *qun'anaya,* which means "zealot." Thus Simon Kananaios and Simon Zelotes both mean the same thing. The first name is a *transliteration,* the latter a *translation.*

Because of his name, many linked Simon with the Zealot Party, the first-century Jewish version of the Palestine Liberation Organization. An ultranationalist group, the Zealot Party engaged in acts of terrorism against the Romans. It was their activity that helped to precipitate the destruction of Jerusalem in A.D. 70, in which more than a million Jews were killed. Some felt that the two men who were crucified along with Christ were Zealots, who, captured by Roman authorities after a terrorist attack, were, in the words of one of them, "paying the price for what we've done." (Lk. 23:41) It is not inconceivable that Simon had at one time been a part of that group which looked to the Messiah as a political liberator. It is quite possible that such a man came to see that Jesus was the Expected One, but that his kingdom was not of this world. Many felt that Jude Thaddaeus was also a former member of the Zealot Party and that Judas Iscariot, too, had been connected with that organization and eventually returned to his former prejudices.

Some legends assert that Simon was one of the shepherds to whom the angels revealed the birth of Christ. Even if he were a boy of ten or twelve at the time, Simon would have been in his nineties or older at the time of his martyrdom at the climax of a very active and vigorous career. Although, contrary to the popular stereotype of people of the ancient world, most of the leaders of the early Church seem to have been vigorous and very long-lived, it is more likely that Simon, like most of the other apostles, was born in the first decade of the first century and was a young man in his twenties when he was called.

Other legends make Simon and Jude brothers, both sons of Alphaeus. This would make them siblings of Matthew and James the Less, and identify Simon the Zealot with Simeon of Jerusalem. This is unlikely since it seems clear that Simeon was not one of the Twelve. Some legends even make Simon a son of James the Less.

Actually, we know absolutely nothing about Simon's background. We do not know where he was born or what his occupation was. The New Testament records nothing about him except that he was one of the Twelve. There is no mention of him by any of the reliable Church historians of the first three centuries. It is quite possible that at one time he was a member of the Zealot Party, but Simon could just as easily have earned his surname through his active dedication to the cause of Christ.

The traditions about Simon's later career are few. St. Basil the Great, bishop of Caesarea, who died in A.D. 379 and is considered one of the major theologians of the Eastern Church, held that St. Simon died peacefully of natural causes at Edessa in Osroene. More common traditions in the Western Church hold that he died a martyr's death in Iran. As to the field of his missionary activity, an obscure theologian named Dorotheus, bishop of Tyre, who wrote around A.D. 300, contended that Simon preached first in Mauretania, then in Africa and finally in Britain. Nicephorus of Constantinople (A.D. 758-829) maintained that Simon was a native of Cana (probably from a misunderstanding of the Greek transliteration) and that he preached in Egypt, Africa, Libya, Mauretania and finally in Britain. Cesare Cardinal Baronio, the Renaissance Vatican archivist and historian, cited material then extant in his archive which showed that Simon visited Britain as early as A.D. 44. Moreover, the Coptic Church in North Africa has a tradition that Simon traveled in Egypt, Africa and Britain, and that he was martyred in Iran. Unlike the case of Matthew, the traditions support each other. If Simon did travel so extensively, it is easy to see why he was called "The Zealot."

If the writings of Dorotheus and others are accurate, Simon must have spent some years in North Africa, gradually working his way westward. Just as the term "Asia" in the first century referred not to a continent but simply to what is now western Turkey, so in those days "Africa" was simply one of several Roman provinces in northern Africa. It occupied only the area of what is now Tunisia. Mauretania Caesariensis included what is now part of Morocco and northern Algeria. Simon must have begun his work among the numerous Jews of Egypt, then moved

146

westward slowly into Libya, then Africa, and then Mauretania. There is no reliable record that tells precisely when Christianity was introduced to North Africa, but it is certain that the Faith had many converts among the Greek- and Latin-speaking intellectuals by the end of the second century. By the time of Constantine, who reigned from A.D. 306 to 337, there were a number of episcopal sees scattered throughout all the African provinces. North Africa remained a bastion of Christianity until the Arab invasions of the seventh century. It is possible that it was through the zeal of Simon and his disciples that Christianity first reached the parts of North Africa west of Egypt, but we cannot say for sure, for the records do not exist.

Britain became a Roman colony in A.D. 43, about a century after it had been visited by the armies of Julius Caesar. We do not know precisely when Christianity reached Britain, but there exists an old legend that shortly after the Ascension, St. Joseph of Arimathea, the friendly member of the Sanhedrin who made his tomb available for Jesus' burial, took the Gospel to Glastonbury. According to the legend of King Arthur, the sinless, invincible Sir Galahad was Joseph's last descendant. Irenaeus, writing about A.D. 176, did not mention Britain in a list of Christian lands, but the African Tertullian, writing about A.D. 200, spoke of "the land of the Britons, not reached by the Romans, but subject to Christ," implying that Christianity was introduced there before Roman rule. He also referred to Britain as a land "where Christ's name reigns."[1]

The Venerable Bede (A.D. 670-732), in his *Ecclesiastical History of the English People,* failed to mention St. Simon or St. Joseph, but noted that during the reign of Marcus Aurelius (A.D. 161-180), Pope Eleutherius received a letter from Lucius, a king in Britain, asking for Christian missionaries.[2] If Lucius was aware enough of Christianity to desire conversion, there must have been some missionary activity in Britain prior to that time. Even so, we are referring to a period about a century after Simon's death.

William Steuart McBirnie suggested that Simon traveled to Britain, but stayed there for but a brief period. He speculated that Simon traveled there around A.D. 60, but was compelled to leave shortly afterward when violent uprisings against Roman authority, led by Queen Boadicea, led to widespread massacres of foreigners. Some early writers believed that Simon had in fact perished there in Britain, but McBirnie felt that it was more likely that he escaped and returned to the Middle East, where he met his end in Iran.

According to numerous traditions, Simon and Jude joined forces around A.D. 66 and moved into Iran, where they met their doom. Before we discuss the martyrdom of Simon the Zealot, it is appropriate to examine what we know of the life and career of Jude Thaddaeus.

*   *   *

Since the eighteenth century, when such a devotion began in France and Germany, St. Jude has been known as "The Saint of Lost Causes." For generations, people in desperate circumstances have asked for the intercession of this apostle. Jude's reputation as a miracle-worker doubtless came from the famous account of the healing of the Prince of Osroene.

As with St. Simon, we know very little about Jude Thaddaeus. He was barely mentioned in the New Testament. The first three Gospels simply mentioned him in the lists of apostles. Some versions of Matthew referred to Jude as "Thaddaeus," others as "Lebbaeus." Mark called him Thaddaeus, while Luke wrote of "Judas, the son of James," and John identified him as "Judas, not Iscariot."

The three names are not as confusing as they might at

first seem. We must remember that the people of the time were often called by a given name, a surname *and* a patronymic. Jude was a given name. The name is Hebrew and is most accurately transliterated as Judah. The Greek form is Judas and the English Jude. This was the name of the founder of the most numerous and powerful tribe of Israel, and was perhaps the most common Jewish male name in the first century. Judas Iscariot and Jude Thaddaeus actually had the same given name. In order to distinguish the "good guy" from the bad, it became tradition to use the Greek transliteration of Iscariot's given name and the English transliteration for that of the apostle also known as Thaddaeus and Lebbaeus.

The names "Lebbaeus" and "Thaddaeus" are, according to most philologists, Greek diminutives for the Hebrew name Theudas. Theudas refers to the heart or breast and means either "beloved" or "courageous." Thaddaeus and Lebbaeus are simply different versions of Theudas, just as, in English, Hal and Harry are diminutives of Henry; Jack and Johnny of John; and Molly, Polly, Minnie and Mamie of Mary. Thus, the apostle whose given name was Judah (Judas, Jude) was also called Thaddaeus and Lebbaeus, perhaps because he (or one of his ancestors) was particularly affable or well-liked, or because he was unusually courageous.

Luke identified Jude as *Joudas Iakabou,* which literally means "Jude, of James." Normally, in the Greek of the time, that meant "Judas, *the son* of James." However, since there is in the New Testament an epistle from *Ioudas . . . adelphos de Iakabou,* some scholars translated the Lucan reference "Judas, the brother of James." Whether the apostle was the same man as the writer of the epistle, or whether James was the apostle's father or his brother, is uncertain. William S. McBirnie maintained that "we can clearly identify" Jude Thaddaeus as the son of James the Great.[3] Other scholars identified Jude as the brother or the son of James the Less. It was, however, entirely possible that the James to whom Jude was related was someone never mentioned in the New Testament. *Jacob* was, like Judah, a common Jewish name.

It is unlikely that Jude Thaddaeus was the author of the Epistle of Jude. This letter was written, probably late in the first century, to warn Christians to maintain orthodox belief and to avoid a particular brand of heresy that was rife at the time. The author of the document wrote, "Remember, beloved, all of you, the prophetic words of the apostles of our Lord Jesus Christ; how they kept telling you, 'In the last days there will be impostors living by their godless passions.' " (Jude, vv. 17-18). This statement implied that the author was writing after most of the apostles had died and that he was not of their number.

Little can be said about the background of Jude Thaddaeus, except that he was related to someone named James. We do know a little about the circumstances of his call. Eusebius wrote that Jude was originally one of "The Seventy" whom Jesus sent out in pairs to evangelize the countryside. Was Jude a member both of the Twelve as well as the Seventy at the same time? It was indeed possible that during the earthly ministry of Christ, the hierarchy and division of His disciples was less rigid and sharply defined than most today would imagine. Jude could have been one of the Twelve, but unlike some of his colleagues such as Peter, James and John, was assigned missionary activity on a frequent basis, in company with men who were not of the Twelve. It was entirely possible that some of the other apostles might have been in this category, too. This might have explained the function of the "Inner Circle," who may have stayed exclusively in the company of Jesus, while others traveled about the countryside.

"Judas, not Iscariot" was mentioned specifically but once in all of Scripture. This was in the fourteenth chapter of St. John. Jude asked Jesus, "Lord, why is it that you will reveal yourself to us and not to the world?" (Jn. 14:22) Jesus responded that those without love for Him could not understand His work. Some scholars seized upon this quotation to infer something about Jude's character. This cannot realistically be done. Paleontologists may be able to reconstruct an entire animal from a mere fragment of jawbone, but it is quite impossible to reconstruct a personality from one rather routine question. About all this passage told us about Jude Thaddaeus was that he was present at the Last Supper and that while the Master was delivering His last teachings before His Crucifixion, Jude was paying attention and asked at least one intelligent question. For all we know, he may have dozed throughout the rest of the evening.

It was probably because of Jude's prior missionary experience that he was evidently the first of the apostles to be sent into the field after the Ascension. As we have seen in the chapter of Thomas, at least according to Eusebius, a Middle Eastern prince had been writing Jesus during His earthly ministry, with the result that the Lord, while declining the ruler's invitation to come in person, promised to send one of His apostles to him.

The prince in question was Abgar V the Black, Toparch of Osroene, a tiny kingdom located between the Trigris and Euphrates rivers. It was important in that a major trade route between Europe and the Middle East ran through it. Sometimes Osroene was allied with Rome and sometimes with Iran. The capital, where Abgar resided, was Edessa, which overlooked a pass crucial to the trade route. A city of great antiquity (now called Urfa), it was ringed about on three sides by limestone hills. It was about 400 miles northeast of Jerusalem as the crow flies.

151

At the time of the Ascension, the twenty-eight-year-old prince, who had been in power since he was nine, was gravely ill — in fact, dying — of "a terrible physical disorder which no human power could heal."[4] Jude immediately left for Edessa.

Eusebius recounted that Jude, who made the journey overland to this inland city, stayed in Edessa with "Tobias, the son of Tobias." It was clear that there was a colony of Jews living in Edessa and that Jude followed the normal procedure for an apostle on a missionary journey when he first addressed the Jewish residents before going to the gentiles. According to Eusebius, Jude "began in the power of God to cure every disease and weakness, to the astonishment of everyone." When Abgar heard about the miracles being wrought among his Jewish subjects, he at once suspected that Jude was the apostle promised by Jesus. Summoning Tobias, he said, "I understand that a man with unusual powers has arrived and is staying in your house." Tobias replied that "a man from foreign parts" had in fact arrived, was staying with him and was "performing many wonders." Abgar requested that Jude call on him the following day.

When Abgar asked, "Are you really a disciple of Jesus, the Son of God, who said to me, 'I will send you one of my disciples who will cure you and give you life'?" — Jude replied, "You wholeheartedly believed in the One who sent me, and for that reason I was sent to you. And again, if you believe in Him, in proportion to your belief shall the prayers of your heart be granted."

"I believed in Him so strongly that I wanted to take an army and destroy the Jews who crucified Him," insisted Abgar, "if I had not been prevented by the imperial power of Rome from doing so."

Jude explained that Jesus had fulfilled the will of His Father. "After fulfilling it He was taken up to the Father."

"I too have believed in Him and in His Father."

"For that reason," said Jude, "I lay my hand on you in His Name." Instantly Abgar, to his own amazement, was healed, along with several other members of his court who were afflicted with various diseases.

Eusebius recounted a further discussion between Jude and Abgar, which he found on record in the Archive in Edessa. Abgar asked more about Jesus, and Jude replied that Jesus had. . .

humbled Himself and put aside and made light of His divinity, was crucified and descended into Hades, and rent asunder the partition which had never been rent since time began, and raised the dead; . . . He descended alone, but ascended with a great multitude to His Father . . . and is seated on the right hand of God the Father with glory in the heavens; and . . . He will come again with power to judge the living and the dead. . . .[5]

If we can believe Eusebius that this was a genuine sample of Jude's preaching and not a fourth-century fabrication, it was very similar to the Apostles' and Nicene Creeds, which were put in standard form only much later than Jude's time. It was a reflection of the unvarying creed and doctrine that was taught by the apostles from the very beginning and handed down orally long before it was ever written down. Jude elaborated on the "narrowing of hell," the idea that Peter would touch upon sometime later by a simple statement in his second epistle that Christ had, after His death, preached to "the spirits in prison." It is also interesting to note Jude's statement that prayers were granted in proportion to one's faith. If we understand this literally, we understand that a spirit of doubt will derail our sincerest prayers. This was in keeping with the teaching of James the Righteous, who declared that a

Christian "must ask in faith, never doubting, for the doubter is like the surf tossed and driven by the wind. A man of this sort, devious and erratic in all that he does, must not expect to receive anything from the Lord." (Jas. 1:6-7)

Jude obtained permission from Abgar to preach openly in Edessa, and began to do so the next day. When Abgar offered to pay him richly, Jude refused, saying, "If we have left our own property behind, how can we accept other people's?"[6] This seemed to conflict with Paul, who wrote the Corinthians, "If we have sown for you in the spirit, is it too much to expect a material harvest from you?" (I Cor. 9:11) Probably the difference was that Paul was declaring that a Christian worker was to expect some sort of material support from those he was serving. Jude perhaps hesitated to accept support from Abgar — even though the prince was now a Christian — because he was unwilling to be subsidized by the state. Although Abgar was at that point ready to perform backward somersaults for the apostle, Jude could perhaps foresee that the time would come when another ruler might demand the right to dictate, in return for support, what the Church would teach — as has often been the case during the two millennia that have passed since the days of Jude and Abgar.

We should be aware that most scholars believe that the materials Eusebius quoted are forgeries. We should also be aware that there is now no way of proving (or disproving) this, since the original documents have long since been lost.

From Edessa, Jude eventually moved into Armenia, which was an independent nation to the north of Osroene. Like Osroene, it was a buffer state between Rome and Iran. In A.D. 63 it became a vassal state of Rome. In A.D. 114 it was annexed briefly under Trajan, only to be accorded its semi-independence a few years later upon the succession of Hadrian. We know little about the evangelization of Armenia in the first and second centuries. The recorded history of the Armenian National Church began around A.D. 300 when King Tiridates was baptized by St. Gregory the Illuminator and proclaimed his country to be a Christian nation. Armenia thus was the first country in all the world to proclaim itself Christian. There had been Christians in Armenia long before Gregory the Illuminator, however, as Eusebius mentioned one Meruzanes, bishop of Armenia, who was in office around A.D. 250. The Armenian Church has always held that it was founded by Jude and that at least four other apostles preached there at one time or another: Andrew, Simon the Zealot, Bartholomew and Matthias. During the nineteenth century Pope Leo XIII invited the bishops of the Armenian National Church to unite with Rome. Bishop Melchizedec Mouriadantz, citing the Church's apostolic origins, replied, "Why should the Armenians go from Apostle to Apostle? What Peter is, the same also is Thaddaeus."[7]

Jude remained in Armenia for a number of years and during that time he was assisted by other apostles and disciples. It was around A.D. 66 that he and Simon, who had evidently arrived from Britain, decided to move into Iran.

Iran, which has often been called over the years Persia (after the predominant ethnic group, just as Great Britain is called England and the Soviet Union Russia), was one of the most powerful nations in the world in the first century. In A.D. 66 it was ruled by Vologases I and was in decline, slowly decomposing into small, semi-independent states. It was a time of violent opposition to all things foreign. Vologases was ardently anti-Roman and furiously opposed to Christianity as an alien doctrine from the West.

The official religion of Iran was then the Zoroastrian faith, founded around 600 B.C. by Zoroaster, who taught a belief in one God and the need for people to act according to ethical principles. In the first century, however, most of the common people still practiced traditional animistic religion. They were dominated by holy men or witch doctors known as *Magi*, who were believed to hold great magical powers.

According to the *Apostolic History of Abdias*, Simon and Jude were opposed in their ministry by Zaroes and Arfaxat, the same two warlocks who had been forced to leave Ethiopia because of the preaching of Matthew. Despite the fierce opposition of these men, Simon and Jude made some 60,000 converts to Christianity in and around the city of Babylon, on the Euphrates River, before moving on in A.D. 79 to the city of Suanir.

It was in Suanir that the Magi, who dogged the apostles' footsteps, persuaded the local rulers to force Simon and Jude to sacrifice to the local deities. Just as the demonic presence allegedly fled the temple of Astamurti in Kalyana in visible form when exorcised by Bartholomew, two black figures were seen fleeing the Persian temple howling furiously. This enraged the Magi further. They stirred up a howling mob which converged on the two elderly men. Jude turned to Simon and calmly remarked, "I see that the Lord is calling us."[8] The crowd began to pelt the apostles with stones. At length a man with a spear came up to Jude and ran him through. Simon was seized by several thugs and was sawn into pieces. According to legend, the careers of two of the more obscure apostles concluded on this bloody and gruesome note.

11

Judas Iscariot:
The man who was a devil
* * *
Matthias:
The austere apostle

IN his poem "Aceldama," Henry W. Longfellow, the sensitive Victorian poet, expresses the feelings of many thoughtful people about Judas Iscariot, the apostle who turned traitor:

> Lost! Lost! Forever lost! I have betrayed
> The innocent blood! O God! if thou art love,
> Why didst thou leave me naked to the tempter?
> Why didst thou not commission thy swift lightning
> To strike me dead? or why did I not perish
> With those by Herod slain, the innocent children
> Who went with playthings in their little hands
> Into the darkness of the other world,
> As if to bed? Or wherefore I was born,
> If thou in thy foreknowledge didst perceive
> All I am, and all that I must be?
> I know that I am not generous, I am not gentle,
> Like other men; but I have tried to be,
> And I have failed. I thought by following Him

I should grow like Him; but the unclean spirit
That from my childhood up hath tortured me
Hath been too cunning and too strong for me.
Am I to blame for this? am I to blame
Because I cannot love, and ne'er have known
The love of women or the love of children?
It is a curse and a fatality,
A mark that hath been set upon my forehead,
That none shall slay me, for it were a mercy
That I were dead, or never had been born.

Too late! too late! I shall not see Him more
Among the living. That sweet, patient face
Will never more rebuke me, nor those lips
Repeat the words: one of you shall betray me!
It stung me into madness. How I loved,
Yet hated Him! But in the other world
I will be there before Him and will wait
Until he comes and fall down upon my knees
And kiss his feet, imploring pardon, pardon!

I heard Him say: all sins shall be forgiven,
Except the sin against the Holy Ghost.
That shall not be forgiven in this world
Nor in the world to come. Is that my sin?
Have I offended so there is no hope
Here nor hereafter? That I soon shall know.
God have mercy! Christ have mercy upon me! [1]

The Unitarian-Universalist poet makes the sensitive reader feel sorry for Judas, who seems to be "set up" by God and the pawn of forces beyond his control, a man who wanted to do good but who was made the "fall guy" in the drama of the redemption of mankind. Longfellow's rosy views of Judas contrast almost totally with those of Dante

Alighieri who, in his *Inferno* placed Judas in the lowest part of hell, among "souls of the lowest class." Here the souls of those "treacherous to their masters" are locked eternally in polluted ice in grotesque and agonized positions in the direct presence of Satan. The devil is portrayed imprisoned in ice, with three faces and mouths dripping bloody froth and pus. In these three mouths are history's greatest sinners: Brutus, Cassius and Judas. Of the three, Judas suffers the most pain, as it is his destiny to have his head and face eternally chomped and crunched in Satan's mouth, while the rest of his body squirms and convulses outside the infernal mouth.

Who was Judas Iscariot? Why did he betray Christ? Why would the Lord have chosen a disciple whom He knew would ultimately betray Him?

We know little about Judas' background. The name Iscariot was a surname, as he was a son of Simon Iscariot. There are two theories about the meaning of that name. One is that his family came from the town of Kerioth in Judea. Most scholars and commentators have concluded that Judas Iscariot was the only Judean among the apostles, the rest of whom hailed from Galilee. Most of the Twelve did, in fact, come from Galilee, but we have no idea where Thomas, Jude Thaddaeus and Simon the Zealot were born. We are on somewhat shaky ground when we conclude, as some commentators have, that Judas betrayed Christ because as a Judean he felt ostracized by a clique of Galileans.

Another explanation for Judas' surname might also cast some light on his character. Some believe that "Iscariot" came not from Aramaic but derives from the Greek word *sicarios,* which means "dagger." These scholars speculate that Judas came from a family of terrorists who took as their surname the principal instrument of their trade. They are led to believe that Judas was a fanatical Zealot who was attracted to Jesus because he expected Him to lead a revolution. When Jesus did not meet Judas' expectations or dance to his tune, the daggerman had no compunctions about coldly destroying his Master. This is entirely plausible, but unprovable.

We can say only that Judas' father was one Simon Iscariot, who seems to have been known to the audience of the evangelists. We know that Judas served as the treasurer for the apostolic college, and according to John, secretly embezzled funds.

Why did Judas betray Christ? This act of treachery has baffled the most learned of experts. Floyd Filson, the eminent biblical commentator, has written:

> Why then this betrayal? Was he jealous of others of the Twelve? Was he repelled because Jesus accepted suffering rather than undertake militant nationalistic leadership? Did he see that Jesus faced defeat and turn traitor to save himself? We do not know.[2]

Before we examine the motive for Judas' treachery, it is well that we recount the facts of his defection, as the evangelists have recorded them. Up to the time of the Last Supper, Judas had showed no sign of disloyalty. He was, in fact, apparently reclining next to Jesus when the Lord announced, with great agitation, "One of you is about to betray me." (Mt. 26:21)

When Jesus said this, each of the Twelve, in horror, asked, "Surely it is not I, Lord?" Judas, too, looked the Master in the eye and said, "Surely it is not I, Rabbi?" Speaking so quietly that most of the apostles did not hear Him, Jesus answered, "It is you who have said it." (Mt. 26:25) Jesus was apparently reclining between Judas and John. On the other side of John was Peter, who asked his friend to find out from Jesus who the traitor was. When

John whispered his query, Jesus, still in an undertone, answered that the traitor was "the one to whom I give the bit of food I dip in the dish." He then gave this morsel to Judas and said audibly, "Be quick about what you are to do." Most of the apostles heard the remark, but assumed that Judas was going out to buy something or give to the poor. (Jn. 13:26-29)

Judas then went to the chief priests and asked, "What are you willing to give me if I hand him over to you?" (Mt. 26:15) Judas promised to lead the temple police to Jesus at such a time and place when there would not be large crowds to protest or resist. In return for his treachery, Judas was paid thirty pieces of silver — the approximate equivalent of $1,200. The fact that the sum was not particularly impressive makes many scholars conclude that Judas' motive was not financial.

At any rate, several hours later Judas led the temple police to Jesus as He prayed at Gethsemane with His other apostles. The Eleven learned later that Judas had arranged a signal: "The man I shall embrace is the one; arrest him and lead him away, taking every precaution." (Mk. 14:44) Shamelessly he came forward, and approached Jesus. "Rabbi!" he said and kissed Him. With no hostility but with great sadness, Jesus responded, "Judas, would you betray the Son of Man with a kiss?" (Lk. 22:48) Apparently His last words to His betrayer were, "Friend, do what you are here for!" (Mt. 26:50) Then He turned to the police who asked if He were Jesus of Nazareth.

John related a curious and awful thing, that when Jesus responded, "I am," Judas, the police and the priests who had accompanied them, retreated a little and fell to the ground. The Jewish Name for God, Yahweh, means "I am." Judas and the priests did not condemn Jesus out of ignorance. Deep within their hearts, even if they tried to shut this knowledge from their consciousness, they knew who He was. Jesus had only to say "I am" for their over-wrought nervous systems to compel them to an involuntary obeisance that their conscious wills forbade.

"Am I a criminal," asked Jesus, "that you come out after me armed with swords and clubs? When I was with you day after day in the temple you never raised a hand against me. But this is your hour — the triumph of darkness!" (Lk. 22:52-53) Despite the resistance of Peter and other apostles, Jesus was led away.

It was then that Judas was stung by remorse. Exactly what happened next is not clear. The accounts by Matthew and Luke do not seem to agree and evidently present but fragments of the full story. Matthew reported that after Jesus had been condemned to death later that night, Judas, who was apparently present at the trial, perhaps even giving evidence that his Master had blasphemed in proclaiming himself God, returned the thirty pieces of silver. "I did wrong to deliver up an innocent man!" he said. "What is that to us? It is your affair!" responded the priests with cold disdain. (Mt. 27:4-5) Matthew then recounted (perhaps condensing events considerably) that Judas threw the money down in the temple and hanged himself. Luke recorded that Peter stated that Judas bought a field with the money and afterward "burst wide open, all his entrails spilling out." (Acts 1:18) We will discuss the manner of Judas' death later.

Why then did Judas betray Jesus? The evangelists failed to provide any information about his personal motives except to say that Judas was diabolical. "Then Satan took possession of Judas," Luke recorded. (Lk. 22:3) Similarly John recounted, "The devil had already induced Judas . . . to hand him over." (Jn. 13:2) According to John, long before the betrayal, Jesus said with reference to Judas, "Did I not choose the Twelve of you myself? Yet one of you is a devil." (Jn. 6:70)

The Scriptures attribute Judas' defection simply to the fact that he was evil and driven — even possessed — by the devil. There are clues that hint that from the very start Judas was wicked, false and hypocritical.

John recounted an incident at Bethany, shortly before the Last Supper, in which Mary, the sister of Martha and Lazarus, anointed Jesus' feet with a costly perfume until "the house was filled with the ointment's fragrance." Judas groused that the money that Mary had spent on the perfume could have better been spent on the poor. John here pointed out that Judas was not really concerned with the poor. As treasurer, he would have preferred Mary to give the money to him so that he could misappropriate it for his own enrichment.

We have here quite an ugly picture. We see a man who appeared stolid and pious, a man who professed a "passion for justice" and a love of the poor, but whose "activism" and "social concern" were simply an "ego trip" and a means of selfish aggrandizement.

Again, at the Last Supper, we see Judas looking Jesus in the eye to protest His announcement of His impending betrayal with wounded dignity. "Rabbi, you surely don't mean me, do you?" He was thus a man who could lie with a straight face. The fact that Judas betrayed Christ with a kiss was especially disgusting. Although disciples normally greeted their rabbis with kisses and men frequently greeted each other on the street in physical ways, Judas' act was still repulsive in that kissing, even if more commonplace than today, was still a gesture of affection and loyalty. Some scholars, in addition, have pointed out that the fact that both at the Last Supper and in the Garden Judas called Jesus "Rabbi" rather than "Master" (as the other apostles did) indicated that he really did not believe in Him.

Judas can thus be seen as a cold, calculating man, hypocritical and dissembling, cunning and double-dealing. He evidently never accepted Christ as Savior even though he knew in his heart that He was the Son of God. It was quite possible that he attached himself to Jesus for some purely selfish reason. He may have been a revolutionary who thought that he could use Jesus for his own purposes and who, failing, turned against Him in a rage and agreed to betray Him for a pittance. Surely the satisfaction of destroying Jesus was greater for Judas than love of money.

Judas did show remorse for his act, but he did not go to Jesus for forgiveness, even while the Master was still alive. He went instead to his accomplices in his dastardly act. Having used him for their unhallowed purposes as Judas had tried to use Jesus, the members of the Sanhedrin had no interest in his plight. Judas' reaction was not godly sorrow, but suicidal despair. If we take seriously the account in Acts, remorse may not have come immediately, but only days or weeks later, after Judas had purchased a plot of ground with the money. He may have tried to return the money earlier, but when he saw that the priests would not accept it, he decided to use it for his own purposes after all.

The portrait of Judas by Longfellow as well as by other sensitive scholars and commentators is not quite scriptural. Many, like the American poet, have tried to humanize Judas and impute honorable motives to him. The British biblical scholar Ronald Brownrigg gently accused John and the other evangelists of "mud-slinging" when they described Judas as a thief and a devil, and suggested that there may have been jealousy on the part of the sophisticated Judas toward the inner circle of "rustic rivals." Brownrigg speculated that "like Martin Luther King," Judas may have "had a dream, and he saw that his dream would be crucified so long as it remained a dream of love rather than practical politics. He may even have felt that

164

he was helping his master to reveal his true purpose for Israel."[3] Similarly, the Scots commentator William Barclay wrote:

> It may well be that Judas never meant Jesus to die. He may well have betrayed Jesus with the intention of forcing Jesus' hand. He may have sought to put Jesus into a position in which, if He was to save His own life, He would be bound to use His power, and where He would be forced to act against the Romans.[4]

Perhaps Judas was a fervent nationalist and patriot, but unless we wish to disbelieve Scripture, we have to accept the evangelists' testimony that Jesus himself said that Judas' motives were not pure and that he was "a devil." This does *not* mean that Judas was not a human being, but a thing from hell cunningly disguised in time and space as a man. It *does* mean that he was a man who knowingly and willingly rejected the authority of Christ. Judas' relationship with Jesus had been so close that his deliberate rejection of Him constituted not a partial (as in the case of most men) but a complete renunciation of divine authority and a total surrender to demonic domination. A man does not have to curse and bellow and froth at the mouth and contort his body gruesomely to be under the power of Satan. Perhaps some of the most thoroughly possessed men and women are attractive and clean-cut, successful and respected, with a ready smile and a sense of humor. Contrary to his depiction by artists and filmmakers who have shown Judas as a grotesque, scowling, leering fellow, he was probably an ordinary-looking man with a friendly, cheerful personality who was able to fool everybody but Jesus.

Still, many are troubled as to why Jesus would have chosen a man that He knew would betray Him. The answer lies in our understanding of divine providence and human destiny.

This problem leads to the overriding one of why there is evil in the world and to the supreme mystery as to why God chose to become a man and suffer and die on the cross and descend into hell. To ask why Jesus chose an apostle who would betray Him is to ask why Jesus came to suffer and die. God ruled that His plan encompassed evil, transforming it through the process of redemption into something infinitely good. Through the murder of His Son, God brought about the redemption of the whole human race. When the evils that individual Christians suffer in their lives, no matter how bitter they are, are submitted into the hands of the Lord, the faithful sufferers are given the promise that, at least in heaven, they shall see these evils one day transformed into blessings that are inconceivable on earth. Thus it was in the case of Judas. Through the deliberate evil of one God-hating man, the Lord was pleased to draw the entire human race to himself and throw open the gates of heaven to all who would receive Him.

But was not Jesus "setting up" Judas? For instance, at the Last Supper, Jesus declared, "The Son of Man is departing, as Scripture says of him, but woe to that man by whom the Son of Man is betrayed. Better for him if he had never been born." (Mt. 26:24) One thing that concerned the gentle Longfellow was whether Judas really had any choice, whether God had deliberately made him evil. This was in fact the belief common in the Calvinist New England in which the poet was raised. It is, however, certain that Jesus did give Judas the opportunity to repent and the opportunity to put his trust in Him. This seems contradictory and illogical. It is not, however, if we realize that we cannot see time in the same way that God sees it. We have true free will within God's will. Calvin wrote that everything was determined at the beginning of the world, even the eternal destiny of generations yet unborn. If God was totally sovereign, the French theologian argued, then free will was an illusion. This is so if we see time as linear — that is, as a line, in which events happen one after the other. If we are able to step outside of time into eternity, where events *presumably* would be seen simultaneously rather than consecutively, we would see that, although God is totally sovereign, He acts within the context of our will as He foresees it. Free will is not illusory. We can make real choices, and God incorporates those choices into His divine plan for creation. Thus Jesus foresaw that Judas would betray Him. At the same time He gave him the opportunity to serve Him and exercise a very real freedom of choice in doing so.

Now, let us consider Judas' death, and also the man who replaced him in the apostolic college. We know that the accounts of Matthew and Luke *seem* to contradict each other. Contradictions in Scripture are, however, often a result of a deficiency of knowledge and insight on the part of the reader than of a deficiency in the text. Let us look more carefully at what the two evangelists said.

Matthew tells us that after Jesus had been condemned, (presumably, although not necessarily before His Crucifixion), Judas was seized with remorse and returned the thirty silver pieces to members of the Sanhedrin. When they refused to accept them, he "flung the money into the temple and left. He went off and hanged himself." (Mt. 27:5) Matthew goes on to say that the Jewish authorities bought, with the money that Judas *apparently* left with them, a field in which to bury the foreigners who died on pilgrimage to Jerusalem.

Luke's version is different. The account in Acts seems to come within the context of an address by Peter prior to the election of Judas' successor. If the words are Peter's, then we must assume that Judas was dead by that time.

But it is not clear whether the account here is a quotation by Peter or a parenthetical remark by Luke.

This account mentions no remorse on the part of Judas or any attempt to return the money. We are told, rather, that with the money he bought a plot of land and then "fell headlong upon it" and burst open. According to this account, the plot became known as the "Field of Blood" not because (as Matthew said) it was bought at the price of an innocent man's blood, but because it was literally bloodied by the disintegrating corpse of Judas.

We have received little clarification from the Fathers of the Church, who seemed to have been completely uninterested in Judas. There was an interesting observation by Apollinarius, bishop of Hierapolis in the second century, who wrote that Judas failed in his attempt to hang himself, was cut down, and continued to live for some time afterward.[5] Papias (A.D. 60-135) left a rather farfetched account explaining the text about Judas "bursting asunder." He wrote that Judas swelled literally "to such an extent that he could not walk through a space where a wagon could easily pass. . . .It is related that his eyelids were so swollen that it was absolutely impossible for him to see the light and his eyes could not be seen by a physician, so far had they sunk from their outward projection." Papias concluded that the bloated traitor retired to a secluded spot where he literally exploded. "Not even to this day can anyone pass by the place without shielding his nostrils with his hands."[6] Another account attributed Judas' death to crushing by a wagon on one of Jerusalem's side streets, too narrow to accommodate both the cart and the immensely fat Judas.

It would seem that Papias, Apollinarius, as well as Matthew and Luke were simply repeating stories that they heard. That this is true of the evangelists does not discredit the inerrancy of Scripture. The Bible is to be read *come scritto* — as it is written. When an evangelist or prophet or some other author delivers a teaching of Jesus or reports something else as fact, we must believe it. When, however, a teaching is delivered in a figure of speech, it is wrong for us to assume that the figure of speech or metaphor is literal fact. St. Jerome, for example, is said to have pointed out that the story of creation was given in the manner of a popular poet. It would be wrong, then, to read the first chapters of Genesis as a geological textbook. Similarly, if we look carefully at both Matthew and Acts, we see that the evangelists, in recounting the end of Judas, especially with regard to the meaning of the term "Field of Blood," were repeating what was being said around Jerusalem. In Acts, Luke spoke of what was "known by the inhabitants of Jerusalem" (Acts 1:19) and Matthew declared, "That is why that field, even today, is called Blood Field." (Mt. 27:8) It appears that both Matthew and Luke were merely repeating popular tradition. It can be assumed that after Judas defected, the apostles had absolutely nothing more to do with him. They heard that he had died miserably and that somehow the money he had been given had been eventually used to buy a field for use as a cemetery, but they really had no interest in his fate.

From the two accounts, one can easily piece together a general picture of Judas' end, however. It may well be that he attempted to return the silver, was rebuffed, then decided to use it to buy land. Then, some days later, overcome with remorse, he hanged himself on the land and was not discovered until days later, after his corpse had fallen to the ground and bloated and burst in the summer heat. The land was then claimed by the Sanhedrin, who converted it into a cemetery. At any rate, concerning the end of Judas Iscariot, we should perhaps adopt the attitude of the nineteenth-century lay preacher Dwight Lyman

169

Moody. When attacked for his belief in the inerrancy of Scripture and challenged to reconcile the Matthean and Lucan accounts of the death of Judas, the wise man remarked, "Why on earth should anybody worry about what happened to a scoundrel like Judas?"

*   *   *

Now we come to Judas' replacement, St. Matthias. He was mentioned only once in all of Scripture, in the account that described his election. Peter insisted that Judas should be replaced by a man who had been with "our company" from "the baptism of John" and who had witnessed the Resurrection of Jesus. (Acts 1:21-22). Two men were considered: Joseph Barsabbas Justus and Matthias. The Eleven prayed, "O Lord, you read the hearts of men. Make known to us which of these two you choose for this apostolic ministry, replacing Judas, who deserted the cause and went the way he was destined to go." (Acts 1:24-25) They drew lots and it was Matthias who was chosen.

The commentator Barclay explained how the casting of lots was a common Jewish custom. "All offices and duties in the Temple were settled by lot." The names of the candidates, he said, were usually written on stones and the stones were placed in a container which was shaken until one of the stones flew out. The man whose name was on that stone was declared elected.[7]

Matthias figured so little in the writings of the Church Fathers that some modern writers have questioned whether Peter did not act somewhat hastily in choosing immediately a successor to Judas by lots. They argue that Matthias must have proved unsatisfactory and that the real twelfth apostle was Paul, who came on the scene several years later. Paul, however, did not meet Peter's first requirement, since he was not a disciple from the beginning of Jesus' ministry or at any time during His life on earth.

We cannot conclude that since we know little about

Matthias that he was therefore a man of little consequence. In any case, we are not altogether ignorant about him.

Eusebius and Clement of Alexandria wrote about Matthias. Eusebius said only that Matthias had been one of the Seventy. Clement identified Matthias with Zacchaeus, who was commissioner of revenue in Jericho when Jesus passed by. A short man, Zacchaeus climbed a tree to get a better view. Jesus, passing, looked up and shouted, "Zacchaeus, hurry down. I mean to stay at your house today." The tax collector gave Jesus a splendid feast and announced there that he was giving half of his possessions to the poor and would repay four times over anyone he had cheated. (Lk. 19:1-9) Clement, however, did not say how he made the identification and critics have pointed out that Zacchaeus did not *seem* to have been a disciple from the very start of Jesus' ministry.

Clement provided an interesting clue to Matthias' character which would indicate that the newest apostle was very much in the tradition of John the Baptist and encouraged great austerity of life. He mentioned the deacon Nicolaus, who had a young, beautiful wife. Shortly after the Ascension, some of the apostles accused Nicolaus of jealousy. Nicolaus brought his wife into the company of the apostles and declared, "Any one of you who wants her can have her." Of course, none of the apostles took him up on his offer! Ever afterward, said Clement, Nicolaus led a life of impeccable chastity and austerity, successfully encouraging his son and daughters to live as lifelong virgins. Clement concluded that Nicolaus lived by the precept for which the apostle Matthias was famous, namely that one should "treat the flesh with contempt." Matthias "is believed," he said, to have taught converts that they must "renounce desire" and that they could not "serve two masters, pleasure and Lord." Matthias, furthermore,

171

taught that "we must fight against the flesh and treat it with contempt, never yielding to it for pleasure's sake, but must nourish the soul through faith and knowledge."[8]

In the scanty apocryphal traditions that survive about him, Matthias is usually identified with Armenia. There was also the tradition that he assisted Andrew in his ministry to the cannibals of Scythia. It was quite possible that Matthias ministered in Armenia and in the area on the north shores of the Black Sea for some years before he returned to Jerusalem, where most traditions held that he was stoned to death by a crowd of hostile Jews around A.D. 51,[9] thus becoming probably the second of the Twelve to die.

12

Conclusion: The importance of the Twelve

IT has become the fashion for many modern theologians to present a picture of chaos and ineptitude among the early Church leaders. Often they present the Twelve as ineffectual bumblers who quickly dropped into obscurity or even lapsed back into Judaism, leaving the Christian Faith to be propagated to the world by a cacophony of strident, clashing voices which were ultimately drowned out by the opinionated and overbearing Paul, who singlehandedly distorted the vague, humanistic ethics of Jesus almost unrecognizably in forging a world religion. The German theologian Walter Schmithals went so far as to deny that the Twelve Apostles ever existed. They were invented by Luke, in his attempt to disparage the work of Paul,[1] he maintained.

The British author Paul Johnson, in his *A History of Christianity,* said that it was misleading to speak of the "apostolic age" or a primitive Church and Faith. To do so, Johnson maintained, was to imply that Jesus "left a norm in terms of doctrine, message, and organization. . ." when there was in fact "never a norm." Johnson said that Jesus held His following together because He was its only spokesman. After Pentecost there was not one voice, but "a Babel of voices." Johnson insisted that Peter "did not exercise powers of leadership and seems to have allowed himself to be dispossessed by James and other members of Jesus' family." As a consequence, the Jerusalem Church was "unstable" and tended to "drift back into Judaism completely."[2] Moreover, he said, the early Church was a "terrifying jungle of scholarly contradictions,"[3] led by men who "knew no more about the origin of the gospel than we do; rather less, in fact."[4] According to Johnson, even Paul, who was "the first person to comprehend Jesus' system of theology," was in "sheer ignorance" of the facts of Jesus' life.[5]

Morton Smith, professor of ancient history at Columbia University, in a book review in the Washington *Post* in 1983, maintained that there were many Gospels in the first century and that all the apostles, including Paul, were so divorced and alien from the modern world as to be completely incomprehensible today. He wrote of the "passionate, primitive sects that spread like herpes through the Roman Empire." He insisted that there were many "widely different Gospels" and that Christian services of worship were really séances for the invocation of spirits.[6]

If the modern theologians are correct, the astounding miracle is how from such a crazy jumble of personal idiosyncrasies, from such a confusion of primitive superstitions, from a class of men so stupid and ignorant that they were in "sheer ignorance" of a man, Jesus, who lived in their very midst, could come a Church for which millions have willingly given their lives, a Church which won over the imperial might of Rome, a Church which all the concerted powers of hell in twenty centuries have not been able to destroy. How different was the witness of earlier Church historians! Before the mid-nineteenth century most of them wrote of the unity of the Church to which ancient doctrines testified. The point of view of nineteenth-century French historian Abbé Constant Fouard was, in fact, common: that the total unity of the early Church was a result of the plenary inspiration of the apostles, to whom the Holy Spirit literally dictated the works which are now found in Scripture, as well as traditions which were handed down orally.[7]

Indeed the Church Fathers of the first few centuries testified almost with one voice to the unity of the Church in the apostolic age. For instance, St. Ambrose (c. A.D. 335-397), the influential bishop of Milan, wrote of how the apostles worked out what we call "The Apostles' Creed" to ensure a unity of doctrine.[8] His contemporary, Tyrannius Rufinus (c. A.D. 345-410), an Italian monk who lived on the Mount of Olives, went into further detail. Before the apostles separated to spread the Gospel throughout the earth, they composed the Apostles' Creed by divine inspiration. "So that they might not set forth a different belief unto them whom they should call to the faith of Christ," they gathered together to compile a "rule" for "future instructions." Meeting as a body, they were "filled with the Holy Ghost" and "composed this abridgment of the truths which they were to publish, and resolved that it should be given as a rule to the believers."[9] We should recall that, according to the story of the conversion of Abgar, the apostle Jude, within a short time of the Ascension, instructed the ruler of Osroene in a formula very similar to that of the Apostles' Creed.

We can always dismiss ancient documents as forgeries and ancient writers as stupid, superstitious fellows upon whom no sophisticate of the jet and computer age need rely. However, if we believe that Jesus was who He claimed to be, it is far simpler to believe that He did inspire the Twelve with a unity of doctrine which they took to all parts of the earth, than to assume that the Son of God assembled a team of men who consistently dropped the ball that He passed to them.

Corrie ten Boom, in a talk at the McLean Presbyterian Church in Virginia in 1975, told a story that reinforces this.

It was about the return of the Lord Jesus to heaven. Corrie recounted that after the angels welcomed Jesus home, they gathered around Him asking about His death, Resurrection and Ascension. "What is it all about?" they asked Jesus.

"The redemption of the world," answered the Lord.

"But you have come back here," said the angels. "How will the world know of it?"

"I have trained my men."

"To evangelize the whole world?" the angels asked.

"Yes, indeed." the Savior replied. "Every corner of it."

"How many men did you train for such a mammoth task?"

"Twelve men," answered Jesus.

"Just a handful! But what if they fail?"

"If they fail," said Jesus, "I have no other plans."

"But is that not a great risk to take?"

"No," said the Lord, "because they will not fail."

* * *

There were disagreements — sharp disagreements — over secondary things such as whether or not pagan converts should be bound to observe the Jewish law and how closely the Christian community should be identified with Israel. This led to a great deal of confusion, heartbreak and even bitterness. Despite these difficulties, the essentials of the Christian Faith were proclaimed uniformly by all the followers of Jesus. There is no evidence to the contrary. If there had been no such unity, Christianity would have surely lapsed totally into Judaism — which it never did — or become hopelessly confused with various pagan cults and sects.

Although the first-century Church was looser and more informal than modern denominations, and although Peter did not exercise the monarchic authority of a modern pope, nor was there a hierarchy of priests and bishops as defined and specialized as in recent years, the Church was unified in doctrine and authority. Although local churches evidently exercised a great deal of independence, they were clearly subject to the authority of the apostles.

Let us take an example from Paul's epistles. In Corinth, some of the women had been addressing the congregations with their heads uncovered. In the Mediterranean world a woman covered her head as a sign of her subordination to her husband or father. Although the apostles permitted women to pray and prophesy (preach) in public meetings — at least under certain circumstances — they most emphatically did not support the equality of the sexes as understood by the feminists of their day or ours. Thus Paul wrote, "If anyone wants to argue about this, remember that neither we nor the churches of God recognize any other usage." (I Cor. 11:16) Again, in the same epistle, Paul excommunicated a man who had been living in incest. (I Cor. 5:1-5) In his second epistle to the Corinthians, the apostle reinstated the penitent offender. (II Cor. 2:5-11) If we consider not only the Scriptures but the testimony of the Church Fathers we see that the Church was not "a jungle . . . of contradictions" or a "Babel" of conflicting voices, but an organization of men and women called by the Lord, people who differed in practical matters but who were united in the Gospel of Christ and had clear lines of authority.

In the first chapter of I Corinthians, we see that the apostles regarded with horror the fragmentation of the Christian community into sects: the Petrine Church, the Pauline Church and the Apollonian Church. (I Cor. 1:10-17) All the leaders of the early Church taught that Christians throughout the world were part of one holy, Catholic and apostolic Church — that is, one Church teaching one doctrine, applicable in its essentials everywhere, linked indivisibly to the teaching of the apostles.

All the apostles, then, were faithful to Christ's charge to "go, therefore, and make disciples of all nations. Baptize them in the name 'of the Father, and of the Son, and of the Holy Spirit.' Teach them to carry out everything I have commanded you." (Mt. 28:19-20) These men devoted many years to spreading the Gospel until at length, with one or two exceptions, all of them were killed for their Faith. All Christians everywhere — Roman Catholics, Eastern Orthodox, Episcopalians, Lutherans, Baptists, Methodists, Presbyterians, Moravians, Quakers, Amish — all owe the essentials of their doctrine to the teaching of the apostles, which was handed down to subsequent generations.

Although the apostles were concerned only that future generations know Christ rather than themselves, it is well for Christians in our day to strive to know as much as we can about these men and appreciate the importance of these twelve men who are the Fathers of all Christian churches, who passed down the teaching of Christ to all subsequent generations, and who are role models for all those who take seriously the command of Christ to carry His Gospel to all humankind, regardless of the cost.

Chapter notes

Introduction

[1]J.G. Davies, *Daily Life of Early Christians* (New York: Greenwood Press, 1969), p. vii.

[2]Alexander Roberts and James Donaldson, ed., *The Ante-Nicene Fathers: Vol. V. Fathers of the Third Century* (Grand Rapids: Eerdmans, 1957), p. 255.

[3]Eusebius, *The History of the Church from Christ to Constantine* (Baltimore: Penguin Books, 1965), p. 208.

[4]Henry Bettenson, ed., *The Early Church Fathers* (London: Oxford University Press, 1969), pp. 32-33.

[5]Alexander Roberts and James Donaldson, eds., *The Ante-Nicene Fathers: Vol. I: The Apostolic Fathers, with Justin Martyr and Irenaeus* (Grand Rapids: Eerdmans, 1956), p. 414.

Chapter One

[1]One should recall that the average height for Romans was only 5'2" and that Julius Caesar, who was Peter's height, was considered "tall."

[2]Henri Daniel-Rops, *Daily Life in the Time of Jesus* (New York: Hawthorn Books, 1962), p. 130.

Chapter Two

[1]Flavius Josephus, *The Jewish War* (Baltimore: Penguin Books, 1972), pp. 292-294.

[2]Alan C. Bouquet, *Everyday Life in New Testament Times* (New York: Scribners, 1954), p. 27.

[3]Eusebius, *The History of the Church from Christ to Constantine* (Baltimore: Penguin Books, 1965), pp. 86-87.

[4]*Ibid.*, p. 88.

[5]Ronald Brownrigg, *The Twelve Apostles* (New York: Macmillan, 1974), pp. 75-76.

[6]*Ibid.*, p. 88.

[7]Suetonius Tranquillus, *The Lives of the Twelve Caesars* (New York: Modern Library, 1959), p. 257.

[8]*Ibid.*, pp. 266-267.

[9]Eusebius, *op. cit.*, p. 108.

[10]P. Cornelius Tacitus, *The Annals of Imperial Rome* (Baltimore: Penguin Books, 1972), pp. 365-366.

[11]Eusebius, *op. cit.*, p. 140.
[12]Philip Schaff, *History of the Christian Church, Vol. I: Apostolic Christianity, A.D. 1-100* (New York: Scribners, 1887), p. 255.

Chapter Three

[1]Ronald Brownrigg, *The Twelve Apostles* (New York: Macmilian, 1974), p. 47.
[2]Edgar Hennecke, ed., *New Testament Apocrypha,* Vol. I (Philadelphia: Westminster Press, 1964), pp. 405-408.
[3]Brownrigg, *op. cit.,* p. 54.
[4]*Ibid.*

Chapter Four

[1]Philip Schaff, *History of the Christian Church, Vol. 1: Apostolic Christianity, A.D. 1-100* (New York: Scribners, 1887), p. 417.
[2]William Steuart McBirnie, *The Search for the Twelve Apostles* (Wheaton, Ill.: Tyndale House, 1973), p. 91.
[3]Eusebius, *The History of the Church from Christ to Constantine* (Baltimore: Penguin Books, 1965), pp. 81-82.
[4]*Ibid.,* pp. 123-124.
[5]*Ibid.,* p. 143.
[6]H.S. Vigeveno, *Thirteen Men Who Changed the World* (Glendale, Calif: G/L Publications, 1967), p. 69.
[7]Eusebius, *op. cit.,* p. 72.
[8]*Ibid.*
[9]*Ibid.*
[10]Jean Danielou and Henri Marrou, *The Christian Centuries: The First Six Hundred Years* (New York: Paulist Press, 1983), p. 12.
[11]Eusebius, *op. cit.,* p. 101.
[12]*Ibid.,* p. 100.

Chapter Five

[1]Philip Schaff, *History of the Christian Church, Vol. 1: Apostolic Christianity, A.D. 1-100* (New York: Scribners, 1887), p. 201.
[2]*Ibid.,* p. 430.
[3]Jean Danielou and Henri Marrou, *The Christian Centuries: The First Six Hundred Years* (New York: Paulist Press, 1983), p. 41.
[4]*Ibid.,* p. 42.
[5]Schaff, *op. cit.,* p. 427.

⁶Eusebius, *The History of the Church from Christ to Constantine* (Baltimore: Penguin Books, 1965), pp. 132-133.

⁷Roland Bainton, *Here I Stand: A Life of Martin Luther* (Nashville: Abingdon Press, 1950), p. 332.

⁸Eusebius, *op. cit.*, p. 129.

⁹*Ibid.*, pp. 129-131.

¹⁰*Ibid.*, pp. 138-139.

¹¹Schaff, *op. cit.*, p. 431.

¹²Eusebius, *op. cit.* p. 225.

¹³Schaff, *op. cit.*, p. 431.

¹⁴Ronald Brownrigg, *The Twelve Apostles* (New York: Macmillan, 1974), p. 122.

¹⁵*Ibid.*

Chapter Six

¹*Washington Post Book World,* Vol. XIII, No. 15 (April 10, 1983).

²Paul Johnson, *A History of Christianity* (New York: Rand McNally, 1966), p. 51.

³William Steuart McBirnie, *The Search for the Twelve Apostles* (Wheaton, Ill.: Tyndale House, 1973), p. 124.

⁴Eusebius, *The History of the Church from Christ to Constantine* (Baltimore: Penguin Books, 1965), p. 141.

⁵*Ibid.*

⁶McBirnie, *op. cit.*, p. 123.

⁷Eusebius, *op. cit.*, p. 151.

⁸Emil Kraeling, *The Disciples* (New York: Rand McNally, 1966), p. 51.

⁹*Ibid.*, p. 49.

¹⁰Eusebius, *op. cit.*, p. 141.

¹¹Kraeling, *op. cit.*, p. 49.

¹²Ronald Brownrigg, *The Twelve Apostles* (New York: Macmillan, 1974), p. 133.

Chapter Seven

¹Eusebius, *The History of the Church from Christ to Constantine* (Baltimore: Penguin Books, 1965), pp. 214-215.

²Montague Rhodes James, ed., *The Apocryphal New Testament, Being the Apocryphal Gospels, Acts, Epistles, and Apocalypses* (Oxford: Clarendon Press, 1924), p. 468.

³*Ibid.*

⁴A.C. Perumalil, *The Apostles in India* (Bangalore: St. Paul Press, 1952), pp. 11ff.

Chapter Eight

[1]Eusebius, *The History of the Church from Christ to Constantine* (Baltimore: Penguin Books, 1965), p. 67.

[2]*Ibid.*

[3]Alexander Roberts and James Donaldson, eds., *Ante-Nicene Fathers, Vol. V* (Grand Rapids: Eerdmans, 1956), p. 255.

[4]Eusebius, *op. cit.*, p. 151.

[5]A. Matthias Mundadan, *Sixteenth Century Traditions of St. Thomas Christians* (Bangalore: Dharmaram College, 1970), pp. 42-45.

[6]Leslie W. Brown, *The Indian Christians of St. Thomas: An Account of the Ancient Syrian Church of Malabar* (Cambridge: University Press, 1956), p. 59.

[7]Erwin L. Lueker, ed., *Lutheran Cyclopedia* (St. Louis: Concordia, 1975), p. 406.

[8]J.M. Farquhar and G. Garitte, *The Apostle Thomas in India, According to the Acts of Thomas* (Kerala: Syrian Church Series, 1972), p. ii.

[9]*Ibid.*, p. ii.

[10]Edgar Hennecke, ed., *New Testament Apocrypha,* Vol. I (Philadelphia: Westminster Press, 1964), p. 451.

[11]Farquhar and Garitte, *op cit.*, pp. 21-23.

[12]*Ibid.*, p. 16.

[13]*Ibid.*, p. 29.

[14]Hennecke, *op cit.*, pp. 453-454.

[15]*Ibid.*, p. 445.

[16]Mundadan, *op cit.*, p. 45.

[17]*Ibid.*

[18]*Ibid.*, p. 51.

[19]*Ibid.*, pp. 61-63.

[20]Farquhar and Garitte, *op. cit.*, p. iv.

Chapter Nine

[1]Eusebius, *The History of the Church from Christ to Constantine* (Baltimore: Penguin Books, 1965), p. 152.

[2]*Ibid.*, p. 210.

[3]Albert J. Edmunds, ed., *St. Jerome: Lives of Matthew, Mark, Luke, and John* (Philadelphia: McVey, 1896), p. 1.

[4]Floyd V. Filson, *A Commentary on the Gospel According to Saint Matthew* (New York: Harper and Row, 1960), p. 1.

[5]*Ibid.*, p. 11.

[6]Eusebius, *op. cit.*, p. 74.

[7]Montague Rhodes James, ed., *The Apocryphal New Testament, Being the Apocryphal Gospels, Acts, Epistles, and Apocalypses* (Oxford: Clarendon Press, 1924), pp. 466-467.

[8]*Ibid.*, p. 460.

[9]Alexander Roberts and James Donaldson, eds., *Ante-Nicene Fathers, Vol. V* (Grand Rapids: Eerdmans, 1957), p. 255.

Chapter Ten

[1]A.G. Gibson, "Early Church in Britain," *The New Catholic Encyclopedia,* Vol. I (New York: McGraw-Hill, 1967), p. 805.

[2]Beda Venarabilis, *Bede's Ecclesiastical History of the English People* (Oxford: Clarendon Press, 1969), p. 25.

[3]William Steuart McBirnie, *The Search for the Twelve Apostles* (Wheaton, Ill.: Tyndale House, 1973), p. 196.

[4]Eusebius, *The History of the Church from Christ to Constantine* (Baltimore: Penguin Books, 1965), p. 65.

[5]*Ibid.,* pp. 68-69.

[6]*Ibid.,* p. 69.

[7]Harold Buxton, *The Armenian Church* (London: Spottiswoode, Ballantyne, & Co., 1919), p. 5.

[8]Montague Rhode James, ed., *The Apocryphal New Testament, Being the Apocryphal Gospels, Acts, Epistles, and Apocalypses* (Oxford: Clarendon Press, 1924), pp. 464-466.

Chapter Eleven

[1]Horace E. Scudder, ed., *The Complete Poetical Works of Longfellow* (Boston: Houghton-Mifflin, 1922), p. 402.

[2]Floyd V. Filson, *A Commentary on the Gospel According to Saint Matthew* (New York: Harper and Row, 1960), p. 272.

[3]Ronald Brownrigg, *The Twelve Apostles* (New York: Macmillan, 1974), p. 213.

[4]William Barclay, *The Acts of the Apostles* (Philadelphia: Westminster Press, 1955), p. 9.

[5]Francis X. Glimm, ed., *The Apostolic Fathers* (New York: CIMA Publishing Co., 1946), p. 386.

[6]*Ibid.,* pp. 386-387.

[7]Barclay, *op. cit.,* p. 10.

[8]Eusebius, *The History of the Church from Christ to Constantine* (Baltimore: Penguin Books, 1965), p. 139.

[9]William Steuart McBirnie, *The Search for the Twelve Apostles* (Wheaton, Ill.; Tyndale House, 1973), p. 244.

Chapter Twelve

[1]Walter Schmithals, *The Office of the Apostle in the Early Church* (Nashville: Abingdon Press, 1969), p. 266.

[2]Paul Johnson, *A History of Christianity.* (New York: Rand McNally, 1966), p. 33.

[3]*Ibid.,* p. 22.

[4]*Ibid.,* p. 23.

[5]*Ibid.*
[6]*Washington Post Book World,* Vol. XIII, No. 15 (April 10, 1983).
[7]Constant Fouard, *Saint Peter and the First Years of Christianity* (London: Longmans, Green, & Co., 1892), p. 232.
[8]*Ibid.* p. 233.
[9]*Ibid.*

Given Name	Simon	Andrew	Simon	Jude	Judas (Judah)	Matthias
Patronymic Surname	bar Jonah Peter (Cephas)	bar Jonah	Quananaya	bar Jacob (James) Thaddeus	bar Simon Iscariot	
Place of Birth	Bethsaida	Bethsaida	?	?	Kelioth, Judaea	?
Year of Birth	Circa 4 B.C.	Circa A.D. 5	?	?	?	?
Married	Yes	No	?	?	?	?
Occupation	Fisherman	Fisherman	?	?	?	?
Evangelism Area	Palestine, Syria, Asia Minor, Rome	Palestine, Asia Minor, Scythia, Greece	Palestine, Egypt, North Africa, Britain, Iran	Palestine, Osroene, Armenia, Iran		Palestine, Scythia, Armenia
Date of Death	June 29, A.D. 67	November 30, A.D. 69	A.D. 79	A.D. 79	A.D. 32	A.D. 51
Age at Death	About 70	About 65	70s?	70s?	30s?	40s?
Manner of Death	Crucifixion	Crucifixion	Mutilation	Impalement	Suicide by Hanging	Stoning

Given Name	Jude (Judah)	Levi	James the Less	James the Great	John	Philip	Nathanael
Patronymic		bar Chalpai (Alphaeus, Cleopas)	bar Chalpai (Alphaeus, Cleopas)	bar Zebedee	bar Zebedee		bar Tolmai
Surname	Thomas	Matthew		Boanergos	Boanergos		Bartholomew
Place of Birth	?	Capernaum?	Capernaum?	Bethsaida	Bethsaida	Bethsaida	Cana
Year of Birth	?	?	?	Circa A.D. 1	A.D. 3	Circa A.D. 3	Circa A.D. 5
Married	No?	?	?	No?	No	Yes	No?
Occupation	Carpenter	Civil Servant	Civil Servant	Fisherman	Fisherman	Fisherman	Fisherman
Evangelism Area	Palestine, Osroene, Armenia, Egypt India, Burma	Palestine, Egypt?, Ethiopia?, Iran	Palestine	Palestine, (Spain?)	Palestine, Asia Minor	Palestine, North Africa, Asia Minor	Palestine, Asia Minor, Armenia, Central India
Date of Death	July 3, A.D. 72	Circa A.D. 90	A.D. 62?	A.D. 43	A.D. 100	Circa A.D. 90	August 24, A.D. 62
Age at Death	Probably late 60s	About 90	About 60	Early 40s	97	87	About 57
Manner of Death	Stab Wounds	Probably Natural Death	Stoning	Decapitation	Natural Death	Crucifixion	Flaying and Crucifixion

Index

[B]

Barabbas — 4
Barclay, William — 165, 170
Barnabas (apostle) — 6, 114
Baronio, Cesare (cardinal) — 146
Bartholomew (apostle) — 8, 9, 108, 110-118, 125, 128, 133, 140, 155, 156
Basil of Caesarea (bishop) — 146
Bede the Venerable — 147-148
Bethsaida — 12, 71, 101, 111
Bilocation — 106
Boadicea (queen) — 148
Boniface of Crediton — 108
Braun, F.M. — 91
Britain, Christianity in — 147-148
Brown, Leslie (bishop) — 126
Brownrigg, Ronald — 5, 164

[C]

Caesar, Gaius Julius — 147
Caesarea Philippi — 19-20
Caligula (emperor) — 45
Calvin, John — 166-167
Cassian, John — 99
Cerinthus — 99
Chariline (prophetess) — 109
Chrysostom, John (patriarch of Constantinople) — 2, 93, 114
Cid, El (and St. James the Great) — 75
Claudius I (emperor) — 45
Clement of Alexandria — 4, 54, 74, 79, 93, 94, 140, 170
Clement of Rome — 3, 9
Cleopas — 7, 68, 75, 136, 145
Constantine I (emperor) — 133, 147

Constitutions of the Holy Apostles — 46, 76-77, 92
Corinth — 46
Cornelius — 41-42
Council of Jerusalem — 42-44, 62, 80, 91
Cyril of Jerusalem — 93

[D]

Daniel-Rops, Henri — 13
David (king) — 113-114
deacons, college of — 40
"disciple whom Jesus loved" — 88-89
Disciples, Seventy — 6-8, 150
Domitian (emperor) — 96, 97, 109
Dorotheus of Tyre — 146
Douglas, Lloyd — 11

[E]

Elias of Damascus — 110
Elijah (prophet) — 20-21, 116
Ephesus — 92, 97
Epistle of St. James — 84
Epistles of St. John — 95-96
Epistle of St. Jude — 150
Epistles of St. Paul — 47, 91, 177-178
Epistles of St. Peter — 51-53
Essenes — 14, 57
Ethiopia — 105, 140-143
Ezana (king) — 143
Euodius (bishop) — 77
Eusebius of Caesarea — 3, 5, 9, 48, 49, 51, 64, 93-94, 105, 123, 124, 151, 154, 170
Eutychiane (prophetess) — 109

[F]

Festus, Porcius — 81

189

Filson, Floyd V. — 139, 160
Five Thousand, feeding of the — 59, 101-102
Forgione, Pio — 106

[G]

Galahad, Sir — 147
Gamaliel — 38-39
Gethsemane, Judas in — 161-162
Gospel According to St. John — 90, 93-95, 111
Gospel According to St. Luke — 7, 34
Gospel According to St. Mark — 49
Gospel According to St. Matthew — 115, 118, 137-139
Gregory the Illuminator — 155
Gregory Nazianzus — 93
Gundaphorus (king) — 127, 129

[H]

Hadrian (emperor) — 109, 155
Haile Selassie I (emperor) — 105
Hegesippus — 75, 76, 77
Hellenists — 39-40, 42-44, 104
Hermione (prophetess) — 109
Herod Agrippa I — 44-45, 61, 73-74
Herod Antipas — 16
Herod Philip — 101
Hierapolis — 107-108
Hippolytus — 4, 7

[I]

India, ministry of Thomas in — 125-134
Irais (prophetess) — 109
Iran — 143, 155-156
Irenaeus (bishop) — 4, 10, 93, 99
Isidore of Seville — 108

[J]

Jacob (patriarch) — 112-113

Jairus — 71

James the Great (apostle) — 8, 9, 15, 25, 26, 45, 55, 68-74, 79, 101, 114, 150

James the Less (apostle) — 7, 8, 9, 10, 68, 73, 75, 77, 114, 135-143, 145

James the Righteous (bishop) — 8, 39, 42-43, 44, 68, 77-85, 90-91, 122, 133, 140, 153-154

Jerome — 4, 92, 100, 114, 138, 169

Jerusalem — 30-31, 83, 120

Jewish Christians — 39-44, 79-80

John (apostle and evangelist) — 2, 5, 8, 9, 10, 15, 17, 25, 26, 28-29, 35, 36-37, 42, 55, 65, 69-70, 71, 72, 79, 86-100, 101, 104, 114, 140, 150, 160-161, 163

John the Baptist — 15, 16, 19, 55-58, 70, 71, 78, 87, 111

John Chrysostom — *see* Chrysostom, John

John Mark (evangelist) — 49, 83

John the Presbyter — 5, 93

Joel (prophet) — 33

Joseph, husband of Mary — 78

Joseph of Arimathea — 8, 36, 147

Joseph Barsabbas Justus — 170

Josephus, Flavius — 31

Judas Iscariot — 6, 8, 9, 10, 25, 31, 89, 157-170

Jude Thaddaeus — 7, 8-9, 10, 68, 124, 125, 144-145, 148-156, 175

Jude Thomas — *see* Thomas

Justin Martyr — 93

[K]

Kalyana — 117, 156

Kibbitz, William — 1

Kraeling, Emil — 107

191

[L]

Last Supper — 24-25, 87-88, 121-122, 160-161
Lazarus — 8, 15, 119-120, 163
Leo XIII (pope) — 155
Levi — *see* Matthew
Linus (pope) — 8
Longfellow, Henry W. — 157-158, 164, 166
Luke (evangelist) — 7, 93, 107, 149, 167
Lycaonia — 114

[M]

Martha of Bethany — 8, 31
Martyrdom of Matthew — 142-143
Mary of Bethany — 8, 31, 163
Mary, wife of Cleopas — 68, 69, 75, 90
Mary, Mother of Jesus — 13, 69, 70, 73, 78, 86, 89, 92-93
Mary Magdalene — 8, 27, 31, 69, 90
Matthew (apostle and evangelist) — 7, 8, 9, 75, 94, 114,
    135-143, 145, 167
Matthias (apostle) — 6, 7, 10, 63, 155, 170-172
McBirnie, William S. — 148, 149-150
Meruzanes (bishop) — 155
Milan, Edict of — 2
Miriam, sister of Philip — 108
Moody, Dwight Lyman — 169-170
Moses — 20-21, 44, 78, 80
Mouriadantz, Melchizedec (bishop) — 155

[N]

Nathanael — *see* Bartholomew
Nero (emperor) — 50-51, 53, 92
Nerva (emperor) — 97
Nicephorus of Constantinople — 146
Nicodemus — 5, 8, 36

Pharisees — 36
Philip (apostle) — 5, 8, 9, 56, 59-68, 96, 101-109, 111, 112, 115
Pilate, Claudia Procula — 36
Pilate, Pontius — 4, 36, 39
Polycarp (bishop) — 97, 99
Polycrates — 100, 107, 109
predestination — 166-167
Pulumayi (Polymius) — 116-117

[R]
Rabban Song — 132-133
Revelation (Apocalypse) — 92, 96-97
Rome fire — 50
Rufinus, Tyrannius — 175

[S]
Sacrament of the Sick — 84-85
Sadducees — 36, 45
St. Andrew's cross — 66
St. Bartholomew's massacre — 110
Salome, daughter of Herodias — 16
Salome, wife of Zebedee — 31, 69, 70, 87, 89
Sanhedrin — 27, 35-39, 74, 81-83, 164, 167, 169
Samaritans — 72
Sarah — 7
Schaff, Philip — 72, 86
Scripture, inerrancy of — 168-169
Scythia — 61, 63
Seneca, Lucius Annaeus — 50
Seventy, The — *see* Disciples, Seventy
Simeon of Jerusalem — 75-76, 136, 145
Simon Kananaios (apostle) — 8, 9, 10, 144-148, 155-156
Simon Magus — 48-49, 104
"Sons of Thunder" — 72-73
Sophronius — 114, 117